WORSHIP SONGS

ANCIENT & MODERN

MUSIC EDITION

THE CANTERBURY PRESS NORWICH

HOPE PUBLISHING COMPANY

Published by

**The Canterbury Press Norwich, St Mary's Works,
St Mary's Plain, Norwich, Norfolk NR3 3BH**

The Canterbury Press Norwich is a publishing imprint
of Hymns Ancient & Modern Limited

**for USA and Canada
Hope Publishing Company, Carol Stream, IL 60188**

WORSHIP SONGS ANCIENT AND MODERN
FULL MUSIC EDITION
ISBN 1 85311 051 5 Spiral
1 85311 052 3 Limp

First published 1992

Cover by Farrows Graphic Design, Norwich

Music and text origination by
Barnes Music Engraving Ltd., East Sussex

Printed in Great Britain by
William Clowes Ltd, Beccles, Suffolk

INTRODUCTION

It was the apparent need for songs of a style that bridged the present gap between the classic hymn and the popular chorus that brought about this new departure in an organisation identified so positively with the traditional world of hymnody and that caused the publishers of Hymns Ancient and Modern to offer this collection of 100 worship songs to the Church.

Worship Songs Ancient and Modern is not intended as a supplement to any previous book, but as an independent source of less formal words and music suitable for most services.

It differs from most song books in one important way: many items have been arranged for 4-part choir, so that the traditional SATB church choir may continue to enrich any worship in which it is customary to use a large proportion of songs.

Words have been set to folk melodies, new words and tunes have been written by established song writers in Britain and elsewhere, and established favourites have been selected from current collections. The book includes the work of writers and composers of many centuries up to the present day and, as with our first hymnal of 130 years ago, this is reflected in the title.

The accompaniments are for keyboard; all can be played on the piano and some are well suited to the organ. Most of the songs have guitar chords added. It is hoped that music directors will adapt the songs to suit their own forces and experiment with solo voices and small groups of singers and players to bring the element of contrast into the performance of the songs.

Similarly, music directors and keyboard players should feel free to experiment with tempi and dynamics. Sometimes a brisk speed will reveal new meanings while a relatively slow speed will underline an air of solemnity.

Hymns Ancient and Modern is grateful to the writers, composers and arrangers who have entered into the spirit of the venture with such enthusiasm, to publishers who have given permission for the inclusion of works already published and to all who have in any way helped to provide a vehicle for heartfelt worship and pure enjoyment.

ALLAN WICKS
LIONEL DAKERS
GORDON KNIGHTS
CYRIL TAYLOR
PAUL WIGMORE

In the final stages of preparation the compiling Committee lost one of its most energetic members in the death of Cyril Taylor. Many old and new songs now appear as the result of his tireless search and delighted discovery of good material.

ACKNOWLEDGEMENTS

The Canterbury Press Norwich thank the owners or controllers of copyright for permission to use their copyright material. All copyright acknowledgements are listed at the end of copyright items. Every effort has been made to trace copyright owners, and the compilers apologise to any whose rights have inadvertently not been acknowledged or acknowledged inaccurately.

COPYRIGHT

For permission to print copyright items, whether in permanent or temporary form, application must be made to the respective owners.

GRANTS

Grants of Worship Songs Ancient & Modern may be made by the publishers to help parishes or groups in the introduction of the book. An application form for a grant can be obtained from The Canterbury Press Norwich, St Mary's Works, St Mary's Plain, Norwich, Norfolk, NR3 3BH. Grants do not apply to U.S.A. and Canada unless by special arrangement with the U.S.A. distributor, Hope Publishing Company of Carol Stream, IL 60188.

TEXT AND INDEXES

The songs appear in alphabetical sequence except where this has been changed to improve the layout. The indexes of authors, composers, first lines and tunes appear at the back of the book.

CASSETTE and COMPACT DISC RECORDING

A recording of several items from the book has been made and cassettes and compact discs will be available either from the Publisher or at Christian booksellers from Word Records under the Langham label.

1   Alleluia

William Boyce

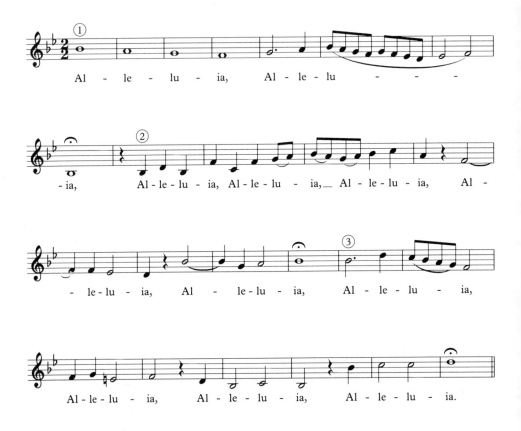

Al - le - lu - ia, Al - le - lu - - - - ia, Al - le - lu - ia, Al - le - lu - ia, _ Al - le - lu - ia, Al - - le - lu - ia, Al - le - lu - ia, Al - le - lu - ia, Al - le - lu - ia, Al - le - lu - ia, Al - le - lu - ia.

Words and music: Reproduced from *50 Sacred Canons and Rounds* (Ed. Kenneth Simpson) By permission of Novello & Company Limited

2   A round for peace

Traditional

Do - na no - bis pa - cem, pa - cem, do - na__ no - bis pa - cem, do - na no - bis pa - cem, do - na no - bis pa - cem, do - na no - bis pa - cem, do - na no - bis__ pa - cem, do - na no - bis pa - cem.

Dona nobis pacem
Give us peace

3 A purple robe

A PURPLE ROBE

David G Wilson
arr Noël Tredinnick

1 A pur-ple robe, a crown of thorn, a reed in his right hand; be-fore the sol-diers' spite and scorn I see my Sav-iour stand. 2 He bears be-tween the Ro-man guard the weight of all our woe; a stum-bling fig-ure bowed and scarred I see my Sav-iour go.

4 He hangs, by whom the world was made, be-neath the dark-ened sky; the ev-er-last-ing ran-som paid, I see my Sav-iour die. 5 He shares on high his Fa-ther's throne, who once in mer-cy came; for all his love to sin-ners shown I sing my Sav-iour's name.

3 Fast to the cross - 's spread-ing span,___ high in the sun - lit air,___

all the un-num-bered sins___ of man___ I see___ my Sav-iour bear.___

1 A purple robe, a crown of thorn,
   a reed in his right hand;
before the soldiers' spite and scorn
   I see my Saviour stand.

2 He bears between the Roman guard
   the weight of all our woe;
a stumbling figure bowed and scarred
   I see my Saviour go.

3 Fast to the cross's spreading span,
   high in the sunlit air,
all the unnumbered sins of man
   I see my Saviour bear.

4 He hangs, by whom the world was made,
   beneath the darkened sky;
the everlasting ransom paid,
   I see my Saviour die.

5 He shares on high his Father's throne,
   who once in mercy came;
for all his love to sinners shown
   I sing my Saviour's name.

Timothy Dudley-Smith

4   An upper room

FOLKSONG

English traditional melody
arr John Wilson

Introduction for verses 1 and 4 (♩ = c.76)

mp

Unison *

1 An up - per__ room did our Lord pre - pare for those he
2 A last - ing__ gift Je - sus gave his own – to share his
3 And af - ter__ sup - per he washed their feet, for ser - vice,
4 No end there is: we de - part in peace. He loves be -

loved un - til the__ end: and his dis - ci - ples still ga - ther
bread, his lov - ing__ cup. What-ev - er__ bur - dens may bow us__
too, is sac - ra - ment. In him our__ joy shall be made com -
- yond our ut - ter - most: in ev - ery__ room in our Fa - ther's

there, to ce - le - brate their ri - sen friend.
down, he by his cross shall lift us__ up.
- plete – sent out to serve, as he was__ sent. (*Introduction*)
house he will be there, as Lord and__ host.

*Any of verses 1–3 may be sung by a soloist or small group, with optional humming accompaniment

Introduction

1 An upper room did our Lord prepare
   for those he loved until the end:
and his disciples still gather there,
   to celebrate their risen friend.

2 A lasting gift Jesus gave his own –
   to share his bread, his loving cup.
Whatever burdens may bow us down,
   he by his cross shall lift us up.

3 And after supper he washed their feet,
   for service, too, is sacrament.
In him our joy shall be made complete –
   sent out to serve, as he was sent.

Introduction

4 No end there is: we depart in peace.
   He loves beyond our uttermost:
in every room in our Father's house
   he will be there, as Lord and host.

F Pratt Green

This folk tune from Somerset is sometimes known as 'O Waly, waly', but it was not in fact sung to those Scottish words. The present words were written for the tune.

5 As Jacob with travel

JACOB'S LADDER

18th-century English carol melody
arr Lionel Dakers

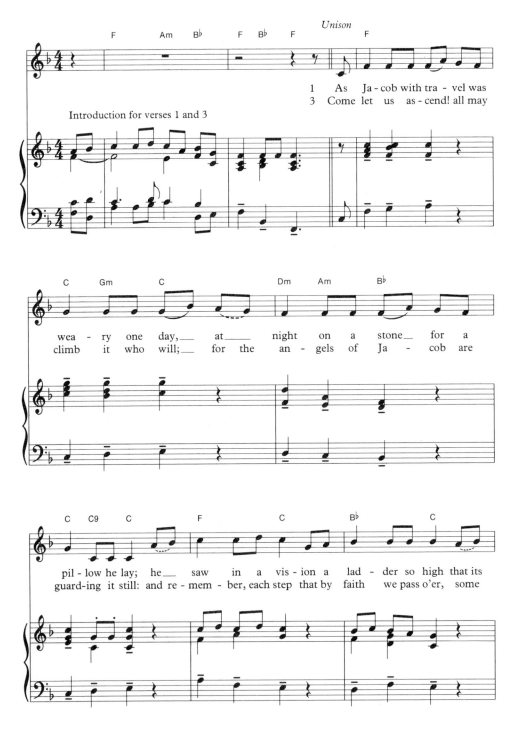

1 As Ja - cob with tra - vel was
3 Come let us as - cend! all may

Introduction for verses 1 and 3

wea - ry one day,___ at___ night on a stone___ for a
climb it who will;___ for the an - gels of Ja - cob are

pil - low he lay; he___ saw in a vis - ion a lad - der so high that its
guard-ing it still: and re - mem - ber, each step that by faith we pass o'er, some

2 This lad - der is long, — it is strong and well - made, has stood
4 And when we ar - rive— at the ha - ven of rest— we shall

hund-reds of years and is not yet de-cayed; ma-ny mil-lions have climbed it and
hear the glad words, 'Come up hi-ther, ye blest, here are re-gions of light, here are

reached Si-on's hill. and— thou-sands by faith_ are— climb-ing it still.
man-sions of bliss.' O— who would not climb such a lad - der as this?

Chorus

Al-le - lu - ia to Je - sus who died on the tree, and has raised up a lad - der of mer - cy for me, and has raised up a lad - der of mer - cy for me.

Return to first page for verse 3

1 As Jacob with travel was weary one day,
    at night on a stone for a pillow he lay;
  he saw in a vision a ladder so high
    that its foot was on earth and its top in the sky:

  Alleluia to Jesus who died on the tree,
    and has raised up a ladder of mercy for me,
    and has raised up a ladder of mercy for me.

2 This ladder is long, it is strong and well-made,
    has stood hundreds of years and is not yet decayed;
  many millions have climbed it and reached Sion's hill.
    and thousands by faith are climbing it still:
    Alleluia to Jesus . . .

3 Come let us ascend! all may climb it who will;
    for the angels of Jacob are guarding it still:
  and remember, each step that by faith we pass o'er,
    some prophet or martyr has trod it before:
    Alleluia to Jesus . . .

4 And when we arrive at the haven of rest
    we shall hear the glad words, 'Come up hither, ye blest,
  here are regions of light, here are mansions of bliss.'
    O who would not climb such a ladder as this?
    Alleluia to Jesus . . .

18th century

6 As the deer longs for streams of water

COLN ST DENNIS

John Barnard

1 As the deer longs for streams of wa - ter, so my
2 O my soul, why are you dis - cour - aged? God in
3 O my God, safe and cer - tain strong - hold, why do
4 O my soul, why are you dis - cour - aged? Why should

soul seeks God the Lord to know; all day
mer - cy hears your an - xious prayer; though his
you seem of - ten far a - way? Send your
you, so nur-tured by his love, be dis -

long, men ask in scorn to see you and my
waves and break-ers have en - gulfed me, I will
truth and light, and as they guide me hear my
- mayed and so down-cast with - in me? I will

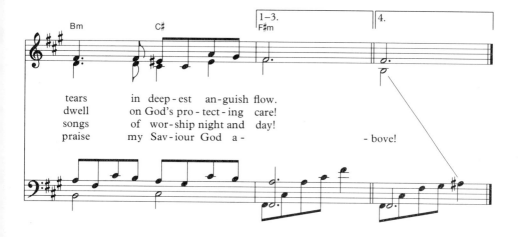

tears in deep-est an-guish flow.
dwell on God's pro-tect-ing care!
songs of wor-ship night and day!
praise my Sav-iour God a - - bove!

1 As the deer longs for streams of water,
     so my soul seeks God the Lord to know;
   all day long, men ask in scorn to see you
     and my tears in deepest anguish flow.

2 O my soul, why are you discouraged?
     God in mercy hears your anxious prayer;
   though his waves and breakers have engulfed me,
     I will dwell on God's protecting care!

3 O my God, safe and certain stronghold,
     why do you seem often far away?
   Send your truth and light, and as they guide me
     hear my songs of worship night and day!

4 O my soul, why are you discouraged?
     Why should you, so nurtured by his love,
   be dismayed and so downcast within me?
     I will praise my Saviour God above!

Paul Wigmore
from Psalms 42, 43

7 At one with God

SHEEP STREET

Cyril Taylor

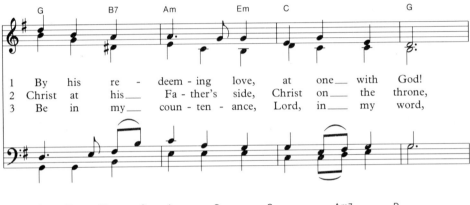

1 By his re - deem - ing love, at one__ with God!
2 Christ at his__ Fa - ther's side, Christ on __ the throne,
3 Be in my__ coun - ten - ance, Lord, in__ my word,

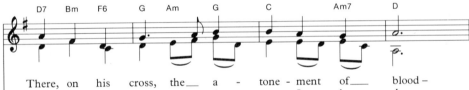

There, on his cross, the__ a - tone - ment of__ blood –
Christ in - ter - ced - ing__ for__ wrong I__ have_ done;__
in my de - ter - min - ing,__ in my__ re - gard;__

Je - sus, who lived for __ me dy - ing that I might be__
Je - sus, who died for__ me liv - ing that I might be__
Je - sus, who came for__ me, set__ my poor spi - rit free__

through all   e - ter - ni - ty____   at   one__ with_   God.
through all   e - ter - ni - ty____   at   one__ with_   God.
in____ life and   death to__ be____   at   one__ with_   God.

1   By his redeeming love, at one with God!
     There, on his cross, the atonement of blood –
       Jesus, who lived for me
       dying that I might be
       through all eternity
     at one with God.

2   Christ at his Father's side, Christ on the throne,
     Christ interceding for wrong I have done;
       Jesus who died for me
       living that I might be
       through all eternity
     at one with God.

3   Be in my countenance, Lord, in my word;
     in my determining, in my regard;
       Jesus, who came for me,
       set my poor spirit free
       in life and death to be
     at one with God.

Paul Wigmore

8   Before we take the body of our Lord

LAYING DOWN

John Bell

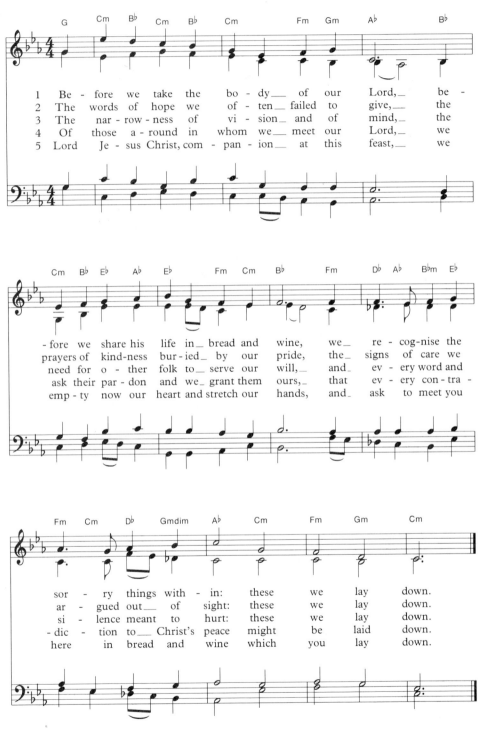

1 Be - fore we take the bo - dy__ of our Lord,__ be -
2 The words of hope we of - ten__ failed to give,__ the
3 The nar - row - ness of vi - sion__ and of mind,__ the
4 Of those a - round in whom we__ meet our Lord,__ we
5 Lord Je - sus Christ, com - pan - ion__ at this feast,__ we

- fore we share his life in__ bread and wine, we__ re - cog-nise the
prayers of kind-ness bur - ied__ by our pride, the__ signs of care we
need for o - ther folk to__ serve our will,__ and__ ev - ery word and
ask their par - don and we__ grant them ours,__ that ev - ery con - tra -
emp - ty now our heart and stretch our hands, and__ ask to meet you

sor - ry things with - in: these we lay down.
ar - gued out__ of sight: these we lay down.
si - lence meant to hurt: these we lay down.
- dic - tion to__ Christ's peace might be laid down.
here in bread and wine which you lay down.

1 Before we take the body of our Lord,
    before we share his life in bread and wine,
  we recognise the sorry things within:
    these we lay down.

2 The words of hope we often failed to give,
    the prayers of kindness buried by our pride,
  the signs of care we argued out of sight:
    these we lay down.

3 The narrowness of vision and of mind,
    the need for other folk to serve our will,
  and every word and silence meant to hurt:
    these we lay down.

4 Of those around in whom we meet our Lord,
    we ask their pardon and we grant them ours,
  that every contradiction to Christ's peace
    might be laid down.

5 Lord Jesus Christ, companion at this feast,
    we empty now our heart and stretch our hands,
  and ask to meet you here in bread and wine
    which you lay down.

John Bell and Graham Maule

9 Be still, for the Spirit of the Lord

Dave Evans

1 Be still, for the Spi-rit of the Lord, the Ho-ly One, is here.
2 Be still, for the glo-ry of the Lord is shin-ing all a-round;
3 Be still, for the pow-er of the Lord is mov-ing in this place,

Come, bow be-fore Him now, with re-ver-ence and fear.
He burns with ho-ly fire, with splen-dour He is crowned.
He comes to cleanse and heal, to mi-ni-ster His grace.

In Him no sin is found, we stand on ho-ly ground.
How awe-some is the sight, our ra-diant King of light!
No work too hard for Him, in faith re-ceive from Him;

Be still, for the Spi-rit of the Lord, the Ho-ly One, is here.
Be still, for the glo-ry of the Lord is shin-ing all a-round.
Be still, for the pow-er of the Lord is mov-ing in this place.

1 Be still, for the Spirit of the Lord, the Holy One, is here.
   Come, bow before Him now, with reverence and fear.
   In Him no sin is found, we stand on holy ground.
   Be still, for the Spirit of the Lord, the Holy One, is here.

2 Be still, for the glory of the Lord is shining all around;
   He burns with holy fire, with splendour He is crowned.
   How awesome is the sight, our radiant King of light!
   Be still, for the glory of the Lord is shining all around.

3 Be still, for the power of the Lord is moving in this place,
   He comes to cleanse and heal, to minister His grace.
   No work too hard for Him, in faith receive from Him;
   Be still, for the power of the Lord is moving in this place.

Dave Evans

10 Bethlehem Carol

Kenneth Simpson

Hear the bells, how they ring for the birth-day of the King, Ding dong bell, ding dong bell.

CODA

Ding dong, ding dong, ding dong.

Ding - a dong, ding - a dong, ding - a dong, ding - a dong.

Ding - a dong, ding - a dong, ding - a dong, ding dong.

When all the voices have sung the round at least once, the Coda may follow

Words and music: Reproduced from *50 Sacred Canons and Rounds* (Ed. Kenneth Simpson) By permission of Novello & Company Limited

11   Bread is blessed and broken

GRACE IN ESSENCE

John Bell

1 Bread is blessed and bro-ken, wine is blessed and poured:
2 Share the food of hea-ven earth can-not af - ford.
3 Know your-self for - giv - en, find your-self re - stored,
4 God has kept his pro-mise sealed by sign and word:

is blessed and poured:
can - not af - ford. _
your - self re - stored,
by sign and word:

take this and re - mem - ber
Here is grace in es - sence –
meet a friend for ev - er –
here, for those who want him –

Christ_____ the Lord.

1 Bread is blessed and broken,
      wine is blessed and poured:
   take this and remember
      Christ the Lord.

2 Share the food of heaven
      earth cannot afford.
   Here is grace in essence –
      Christ the Lord.

3 Know yourself forgiven,
      find yourself restored,
   meet a friend for ever –
      Christ the Lord.

4 God has kept his promise
      sealed by sign and word:
   here, for those who want him –
      Christ the Lord.

John Bell and Graham Maule

12 Christ be beside me

BUNESSAN

Gaelic melody

1 Christ be beside me,
  Christ be before me,
Christ be behind me,
  King of my heart.
Christ be within me,
  Christ be below me,
Christ be above me,
  never to part.

2 Christ on my right hand,
  Christ on my left hand,
Christ all around me,
  shield in the strife.
Christ in my sleeping,
  Christ in my sitting,
Christ in my rising,
  light of my life.

3 Christ be in all hearts
  thinking about me,
Christ be in all tongues
  telling of me.
Christ be the vision
  in eyes that see me,
in ears that hear me,
  Christ ever be.

James Quinn S J
from 'St Patrick's Breastplate'

13   Christ in the stranger's guise

THE LEAVING OF LIVERPOOL

Irish traditional melody
arr Lionel Dakers

1 From heaven to here— and from
2 The folk who jour-ney on the
3 The love that's shared a-long the
4 From heaven to here— and from

here to heaven is a dis - tance less than tis - sue
road with Christ are the ones who've left their selves be -
roy - al road is a love not found when stand - ing
here to heaven is a dis - tance less than tis - sue

thin, and it's trod by him who in the stran - ger's guise is made
- hind. Their song is taught them by the deaf and dumb, their ho -
still. It— lives and grows wher - e - ver faith is known as a
thin, and it's trod by those who meet the ris - en Christ as a

will be done by the peo-ple you've loved and you've led.

1 From heaven to here and from here to heaven
    is a distance less than tissue thin,
  and it's trod by him who in the stranger's guise
    is made known when he is welcomed in:

      So come, Lord Christ, in the stranger's guise,
        known both through scriptures and through broken bread.
      Your kingdom come and on the earth your will be done
        by the people you've loved and you've led.

2 The folk who journey on the road with Christ
    are the ones who've left their selves behind.
  Their song is taught them by the deaf and dumb,
    their horizon is shown by the blind:
      So come, Lord Christ . . .

3 The love that's shared along the royal road
    is a love not found when standing still.
  It lives and grows wherever faith is known
    as a movement grounded in God's will.
      So come, Lord Christ . . .

4 From heaven to here and from here to heaven
    is a distance less than tissue thin,
  and it's trod by those who meet the risen Christ
    as a stranger to be welcomed in.
      So come, Lord Christ . . .

                                        John Bell and Graham Maule

14 Christ triumphant, ever reigning

GUITING POWER

John Barnard

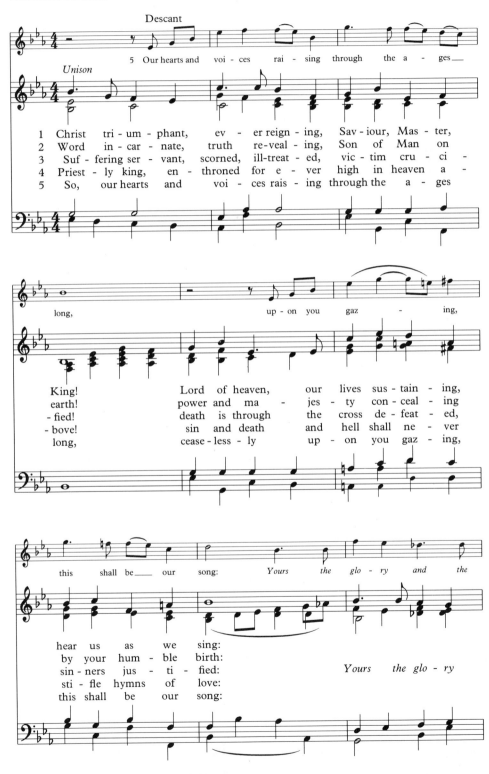

Descant

5 Our hearts and voi - ces rai - sing through the a - ges___

Unison

1 Christ tri - um - phant, ev - er reign - ing, Sav - iour, Mas - ter, King!
2 Word in - car - nate, truth re-veal - ing, Son of Man on earth!
3 Suf - fering ser - vant, scorned, ill-treat - ed, vic - tim cru - ci - fied!
4 Priest - ly king, en - throned for e - ver high in heaven a - bove!
5 So, our hearts and voi - ces rais - ing through the a - ges long,

long,
up - on you gaz - ing,

King!   Lord of heaven,   our lives sus - tain - ing,
earth!   power and ma - jes - ty con - ceal - ing
- fied!   death is through the cross de - feat - ed,
- bove!   sin and death and hell shall ne - ver
long,   cease - less - ly up - on you gaz - ing,

this shall be___ our song: *Yours the glo - ry and the*

hear us as we sing:
by your hum - ble birth:
sin - ners jus - ti - fied:
sti - fle hymns of love:
this shall be our song:

Yours the glo - ry

crown, the high re - nown,_____ the e - ter - nal name!

and the crown, the high re-nown, the e - ter - nal name!

HARMONY SETTING FOR VERSE 4

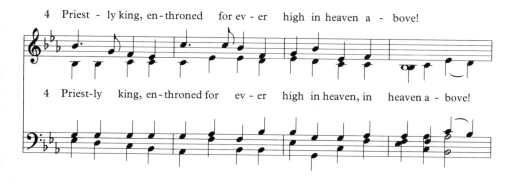

4 Priest - ly king, en - throned for ev - er high in heaven a - bove!

4 Priest-ly king, en - throned for ev - er high in heaven, in heaven a - bove!

sin and death and hell shall ne - ver sti - fle hymns of love:

sin and death and hell shall ne - ver sti - fle hymns of love:

Yours the

Yours the

Yours the glo-ry and the crown, the high re-nown, the e-ter - nal name!

glo - ry and the crown, the high re - nown, the e-ter - nal name!
Yours the glo-ry

glo - ry

1 Christ triumphant, ever reigning,
      Saviour, Master, King!
   Lord of heaven, our lives sustaining,
      hear us as we sing:

      *Yours the glory and the crown,
         the high renown, the eternal name!*

2 Word incarnate, truth revealing,
      Son of Man on earth!
   power and majesty concealing
      by your humble birth:
      Yours the glory . . .

3 Suffering servant, scorned, ill-treated,
      victim crucified!
   death is through the cross defeated,
      sinners justified:
      Yours the glory . . .

4 Priestly king, enthroned for ever
      high in heaven above!
   sin and death and hell shall never
      stifle hymns of love:
      Yours the glory . . .

5 So, our hearts and voices raising
      through the ages long,
   ceaselessly upon you gazing,
      this shall be our song:
      Yours the glory . . .

                              Michael Saward

15 A Christmas round

Kenneth Simpson

Glo - - - ria__ in_ ex - cel - sis._ De - o.

CODA

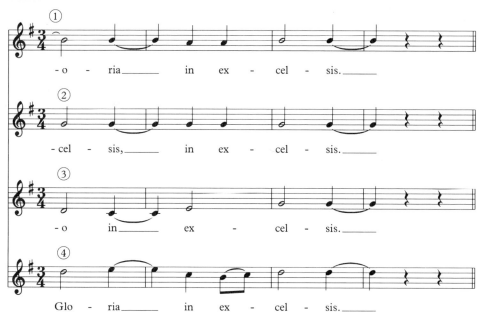

-o - ria_____ in ex - cel - sis._____

- cel - sis,_____ in ex - cel - sis._____

-o in_____ ex - cel - sis._____

Glo - ria_____ in ex - cel - sis._____

When all voices have sung the round at least once, the Coda may follow

Gloria in excelsis Deo
Glory to God in the highest

Words and music: Reproduced from *50 Sacred Canons and Rounds* (Ed. Kenneth Simpson) By permission of Novello & Company Limited

16 Come quickly, Lord!

WINSON

John Barnard

Lyrics under the music (verses 1–4):

1. 'Come quickly, Lord!' they prayed, faithful, though still afraid; in death proclaiming Christ would come again, as he had said.

2. To this the Church has clung through centuries of wrong, crying, despite false prophecies: How long, O Lord, how long?

3. Were you to come today, our lives in disarray, would we not plead with you, as Peter did, to go away?

4. Yet we, like Peter, know you would not, could not go; nor need we wait until the end of time to prove it so.

1 'Come quickly, Lord!' they prayed,
faithful, though still afraid;
in death proclaiming Christ
   would come again,
as he had said.

2 To this the Church has clung
through centuries of wrong,
crying, despite false prophecies: How long,
O Lord, how long?

3 Were you to come today,
our lives in disarray,
would we not plead with you,
   as Peter did,
to go away?

4 Yet we, like Peter, know
you would not, could not go;
nor need we wait until the end of time
to prove it so.

F Pratt Green

17 Comes Mary to the grave

CHURCH CLOSE

David Iliff

1 Comes Ma-ry to the grave;— no sing-ing bird has spo - ken, nor
2 Says Je-sus at her side,— no long-er Je - sus dy - ing, 'Why,
3 With Ma-ry on this day— we join our voi-ces, prais - ing the

has the world a - wo - ken, and in her grief all love lies lost and bro-ken.
Ma-ry, are you cry - ing?' She turns, with joy, 'My Lord! my love!' re - ply-ing.
God of Je-sus' rais-ing, and sing the tri-umph of that love a - maz-ing.

1 Comes Mary to the grave;
   no singing bird has spoken,
nor has the world awoken,
   and in her grief all love lies lost and broken.

2 Says Jesus at her side,
   no longer Jesus dying,
'Why, Mary, are you crying?'
   She turns, with joy, 'My Lord! my love!' replying.

3 With Mary on this day
   we join our voices, praising
the God of Jesus' raising,
   and sing the triumph of that love amazing.

Michael Perry
from St John: 20

18 Dark the night

STREET END

Cyril Taylor

Unison

1 Dark the night, but joy comes in the
2 God has turned our cry-ing in-to

morn-ing,—   sha-dows fly be-fore the ris-ing sun;
danc-ing,—   praise him for the bat-tles he has won;

God is shin-ing! See his love and   mer - cy   flood our
dark the night, but joy comes in the   morn - ing,   sha-dows

hearts with light where there was none.
fly be-fore the ris - ing sun.

1 Dark the night, but joy comes in the morning,
        shadows fly before the rising sun;
    God is shining! See his love and mercy
        flood our hearts with light where there was none.

2 God has turned our crying into dancing,
        praise him for the battles he has won;
    dark the night, but joy comes in the morning,
        shadows fly before the rising sun.

Paul Wigmore
from Psalm 30: 4

19 Day by day

DAY BY DAY

Martin How

Moving easily

mp

Day by day, dear Lord, of thee three things I

pray.

To see thee more clear - ly, love thee more dear - ly,

Fol-low thee more near - ly, day by day.

Day by day, dear Lord,
of thee three things I pray.
To see thee more clearly,
love thee more dearly,
Follow thee more nearly,
day by day.

Prayer of St Richard of Chichester

20　Doxology canon

Gerald S Henderson

Praise God, from whom all bless-ings flow, praise him, all crea-tures here___ be - low; praise him a - bove, ye heaven - ly___ host, praise Fa - ther,_ Son and Ho - ly Ghost.

Praise God, from whom all blessings flow,
praise him, all creatures here below;
praise him above, ye heavenly host,
praise Father, Son and Holy Ghost.

Thomas Ken

Music: © 1986 Word Music (a division of Word Inc) Word Music (UK) (a division of Word (UK) Ltd), 9 Holdom Avenue, Bletchley, Milton Keynes, MK1 1QR, England.
International Copyright secured. Used by permission

21 Easter canon

Gumpelzhaimer

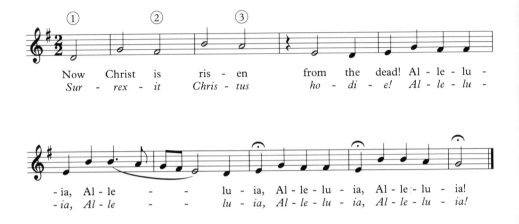

Now Christ is ris - en from the dead! Al - le - lu -
Sur - rex - it Chris - tus ho - di - e! Al - le - lu -

- ia, Al - le - - - lu - ia, Al - le - lu - ia, Al - le - lu - ia!
- ia, Al - le - - - lu - ia, Al - le - lu - ia, Al - le - lu - ia!

Now Christ is risen from the dead!
Alleluia, Alleluia, Alleluia, Alleluia!

Surrexit Christus hodie!
Alleluia, Alleluia, Alleluia, Alleluia!

Words and music: Reproduced from *50 Sacred Canons and Rounds* (Ed. Kenneth Simpson) By permission of Novello & Company Limited

22 Easter song of praise

WOODLANDS   Walter Greatorex

1 Sing choirs of heaven! Let saints and an-gels sing! A-round God's
2 Sing choirs of earth! Be-hold, your light has come! The glo - ry
3 Sing Church of God! Ex - ult with joy out-poured! The gos - pel

throne ex - ult in har - mo - ny! Now Je - sus Christ is
of the Lord shines ra - diant - ly! Lift up your hearts, for
trum-pets tell of vic - tory won! Your Sav-iour lives: he's

ris - en from the grave! Sa - lute your King in glo-rious sym - pho-ny!
Christ has con-quered death! The night is past; the day of life is here!
with you ev - er - more! Let all God's peo-ple shout the long A - men!

1   Sing choirs of heaven! Let saints and angels sing!
    Around God's throne exult in harmony!
    Now Jesus Christ is risen from the grave!
    Salute your King in glorious symphony!

2   Sing choirs of earth! Behold, your light has come!
    The glory of the Lord shines radiantly!
    Lift up your hearts, for Christ has conquered death!
    The night is past; the day of life is here!

3   Sing Church of God! Exult with joy outpoured!
    The gospel trumpets tell of victory won!
    Your Saviour lives: he's with you evermore!
    Let all God's people shout the long Amen!

The Easter Song of Praise

23   Exult, creation round God's throne

FENNY STRATFORD

Paul Edwards

Unison

1 Ex - ult, cre - a - tion round God's throne! All heaven, re -
(*Optional*) 4 Ex - ult in God, pure well of truth; in Christ, fresh

- joice! All an - gels, sing! Sal - va - tion's trum - pet
foun - tain - head of grace; in Spi - rit, flow - ing

sound a - loud for Je - sus Christ, our ris - en king.
stream of life – e - ter - nal Joy our hearts em - brace.

Harmony

2 Ex - ult, O earth, in ra - diant hope; in Christ's ma -
3 Ex - ult, all Christ - ians, one in praise with our Je -

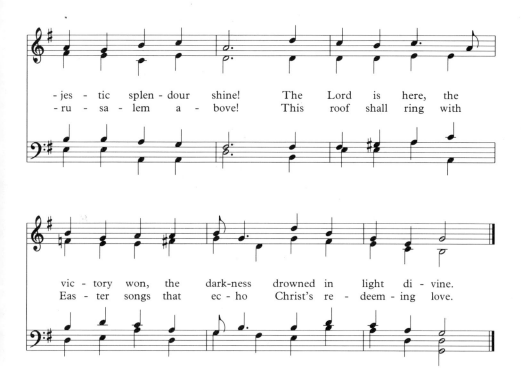

-jes - tic splen - dour shine! The Lord is here, the
-ru - sa - lem a - bove! This roof shall ring with

vic - tory won, the dark-ness drowned in light di - vine.
Eas - ter songs that ec - ho Christ's re - deem - ing love.

1 Exult, creation round God's throne!
All heaven, rejoice! All angels, sing!
Salvation's trumpet sound aloud
for Jesus Christ, our risen king.

2 Exult, O earth, in radiant hope;
in Christ's majestic splendour shine!
The Lord is here, the victory won,
the darkness drowned in light divine.

3 Exult, all Christians, one in praise
with our Jerusalem above!
This roof shall ring with Easter songs
that echo Christ's redeeming love.

Optional verse

4 Exult in God, pure well of truth;
in Christ, fresh fountainhead of grace;
in Spirit, flowing stream of life –
eternal Joy our hearts embrace.

Christopher Idle
from The Easter Song of Praise

24 Everlasting love

CHILDREN

John Dankworth

1 Ev - er-last-ing Fa - ther, the Prince of Peace,
2 There's a new di - men - sion of love sub-lime,

Peacefully

born as Christ our Sav - iour, and shall we cease, now we are
far be-yond all ques - tion of space and time; out-side our

his, saved by his grace, prais-ing the name of Je - sus?
world, in-side our heart, mys-tery of grace and mer - cy:

Chorus

(echo)

Ev - er - last - ing love! No be - gin - ning, ne - ver end - ing,
(Ev - er - last - ing love!)

Rhythmically

mf

all the past of our of - fend - ing ta - ken on his Cross;

(echo)

Ev - er - last - ing love! From a vast e - ter - ni - ty a -
(Ev - er - last - ing love!)

- bove Je - sus calls us to him, cir - cles of love from the Fa - ther through him,

ev - er-last - ing   love!   praise the Lord in   the light of his

1. love! _____   2. love! _____

1 Everlasting Father,
       the Prince of Peace,
   born as Christ our Saviour,
       and shall we cease,
           now we are his,
           saved by his grace,
           praising the name of Jesus?

   Everlasting love!
   No beginning, never ending,
       all the past of our offending taken on his Cross;
   Everlasting love!
   From a vast eternity above
       Jesus calls us to him,
       circles of love from the Father through him,
   everlasting love!
       praise the Lord in the light of his love!

2 There's a new dimension
       of love sublime,
   far beyond all question
       of space and time;
           outside our world,
           inside our heart,
           mystery of grace and mercy:
   Everlasting love . . .

                                        Paul Wigmore

25 Father in heaven

HARROW WEALD

John Barnard

1 Fa - ther in hea - ven, grant to your child - ren mer - cy and bless - ing,
2 Je - sus, re-deem - er, may we re - mem - ber your gra-cious pas - sion,
3 Spi - rit des-cen - ding, whose is the bless - ing, strength for the wea - ry,

songs ne - ver ceas - ing; love to u - nite us,
your re - sur - rec - tion: wor - ship we bring you,
help for the need - y: sealed in our son - ship,

grace to re-deem us, Fa - ther in hea - ven, Fa - ther, our God.
praise we shall sing you, Je - sus, re-deem - er. Je - sus, our Lord.
yours be our wor - ship, Spi - rit des-cend - ing, Spi - rit a-dored.

1 Father in heaven,
    grant to your children
mercy and blessing,
songs never ceasing;
love to unite us,
grace to redeem us,
Father in heaven,
Father, our God.

2 Jesus, redeemer,
    may we remember
your gracious passion,
your resurrection:
worship we bring you,
praise we shall sing you,
Jesus, redeemer.
Jesus, our Lord.

3 Spirit descending,
    whose is the blessing,
strength for the weary,
help for the needy:
sealed in our sonship,
yours be our worship,
Spirit descending,
Spirit adored.

D T Niles

26   Fairest Lord Jesus

FAIREST LORD JESUS

Silesian folk song
arr Martin How

Moderato

1 Fair - est Lord Je - sus, Lord of all cre - a - tion, Je - sus, of

God and__ Ma - ry the Son; thee will I

cher - ish, thee will I hon - our, O thou my

soul's de - light and crown.

Harmony

2 Fair are the mea - dows, fair-er still the wood - lands, robed in the

ver - dure and bloom of___ spring. Je - sus is fair - er,

Je - sus is pur - er,___ he___ makes the sad - dest___ heart to___

sing.

3 Fair are the flow-ers, fair-er still the
sons of men, in all the fresh-ness of youth ar - rayed:
yet is their beau - ty fa - ding and fleet - ing; my Je-sus,

1 Fairest Lord Jesus,
    Lord of all creation,
Jesus, of God and Mary the Son;
    thee will I cherish, thee will I honour,
O thou my soul's delight and crown.

2 Fair are the meadows,
    fairer still the woodlands,
robed in the verdure and bloom of spring.
    Jesus is fairer, Jesus is purer,
he makes the saddest heart to sing.

3 Fair are the flowers,
    fairer still the sons of men,
in all the freshness of youth arrayed:
    yet is their beauty fading and fleeting;
my Jesus, thine will never fade.

German 17th century
tr Lilian S Stevenson

27 Father God in heaven

KUM BA YAH

Traditional melody
arr Gabriel Jackson

Unison

1 Fa - ther God in heaven, Lord most high: hear your
2 May your king - dom come here on earth; may your
3 Give us dai - ly bread day by day, and for -
4 Lead us in your way, make us strong; when temp -
5 All things come from you, all are yours – king - dom,

child - ren's prayer, Lord most high: hal-lowed be your name, Lord most
will be done here on earth, as it is in heaven so on
- give our sins day by day, as we too for - give day by
- ta - tions come make us strong; save us all from sin, keep us
glo - ry, power, all are yours; take our lives and gifts, all are

high – O Lord,___ hear our prayer.
earth – O Lord,___ hear our prayer.
day – O Lord,___ hear our prayer.
strong – O Lord,___ hear our prayer.
yours – O Lord,___ hear our prayer.

1 Father God in heaven, Lord most high:
  hear your children's prayer, Lord most high:
 hallowed be your name, Lord most high –
  O Lord, hear our prayer.

2 May your kingdom come here on earth;
  may your will be done here on earth,
 as it is in heaven so on earth –
  O Lord, hear our prayer.

3 Give us daily bread day by day,
  and forgive our sins day by day,
 as we too forgive day by day –
  O Lord, hear our prayer.

4 Lead us in your way, make us strong;
  when temptations come make us strong;
 save us all from sin, keep us strong –
  O Lord, hear our prayer.

5 All things come from you, all are yours –
  kingdom, glory, power, all are yours;
 take our lives and gifts, all are yours –
  O Lord, hear our prayer.

J E Seddon
from The Lord's Prayer

28 Father, we adore you

T Coelho

Slowly and sustained

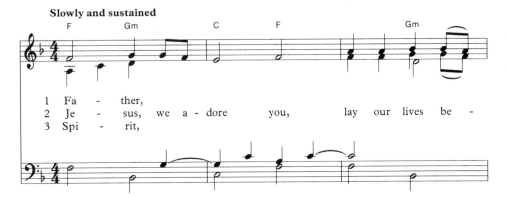

1 Fa - ther,
2 Je - sus, we a - dore you, lay our lives be -
3 Spi - rit,

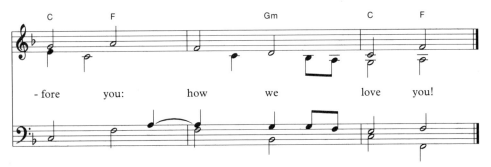

- fore you: how we love you!

This item may be sung as a 3-part round.

1 Father, we adore you,
   lay our lives before you:
   how we love you!

2 Jesus, we adore you,
   lay our lives before you:
   how we love you!

3 Spirit, we adore you,
   lay our lives before you:
   how we love you!

T Coelho

29 Gather us in

GATHER US IN

Marty Haugen

1 Here in this place the new light is stream-ing, now is the dark - ness
2 We are the young, our lives are a mys - t'ry, we are the old who
3 Here we will take the wine and the wa - ter, here we will take the
4 Ga-ther us in and hold us for ev - er, ga-ther us in and

van-ished a - way: see in this space our fears and our dream-ings
yearn for your face; we have been sung through-out all of his - t'ry,
bread of new birth: here you shall call your sons and your daugh-ters,
make us your own, ga-ther us in, all peo-ples to - ge - ther,

brought here to you in the light of this day. _____
called to be light to the whole hu-man race. _____
call us a - new to be salt for the earth. _____
fire of your love in our flesh and our bone. _____

1 Here in this place the new light is streaming,
    now is the darkness vanished away:
see in this space our fears and our dreamings
    brought here to you in the light of this day.
Gather us in, the lost and forsaken,
    gather us in, the blind and the lame:
call to us now and we shall awaken,
    we shall arise at the sound of our name.

2 We are the young, our lives are a myst'ry,
    we are the old who yearn for your face;
we have been sung throughout all of hist'ry,
    called to be light to the whole human race.
Gather us in, the rich and the haughty,
    gather us in, the proud and the strong:
give us a heart so meek and so lowly,
    give us the courage to enter the song.

3 Here we will take the wine and the water,
    here we will take the bread of new birth:
here you shall call your sons and your daughters,
    call us anew to be salt for the earth.
Give us to drink the wine of compassion,
    give us to eat the bread that is you:
nourish us well and teach us to fashion
    lives that are holy and hearts that are true.

4 Gather us in and hold us for ever,
    gather us in and make us your own,
gather us in, all peoples together,
    fire of your love in our flesh and our bone.
Not in the dark of buildings confining,
    not in some heaven light-years away,
here in this place the new light is shining,
    now is the kingdom, and now is the day.

Marty Haugen

30 God in his love for us

JULIAN OF NORWICH

David Ashley White

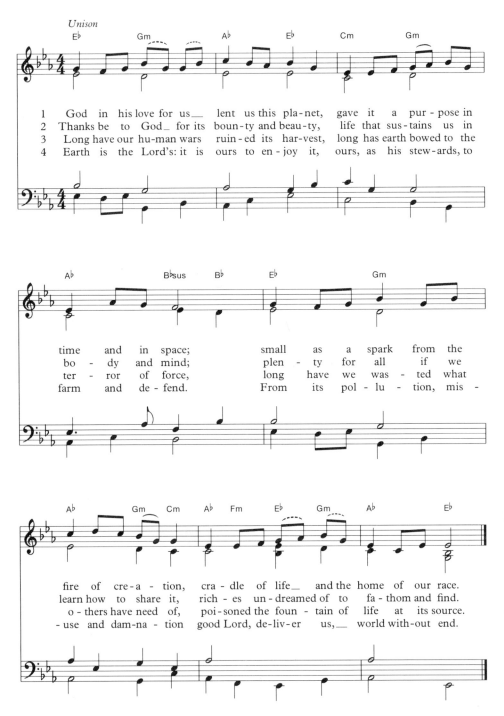

1 God in his love for us— lent us this pla-net, gave it a pur-pose in time and in space; small as a spark from the fire of cre-a-tion, cra-dle of life— and the home of our race.

2 Thanks be to God— for its boun-ty and beau-ty, life that sus-tains us in bo-dy and mind; plen-ty for all if we learn how to share it, rich-es un-dreamed of to fa-thom and find.

3 Long have our hu-man wars ruin-ed its har-vest, long has earth bowed to the ter-ror of force, long have we was-ted what o-thers have need of, poi-soned the foun-tain of life at its source.

4 Earth is the Lord's: it is ours to en-joy it, ours, as his stew-ards, to farm and de-fend. From its pol-lu-tion, mis-use and dam-na-tion good Lord, de-liv-er us,— world with-out end.

1 God in his love for us lent us this planet,
       gave it a purpose in time and in space;
   small as a spark from the fire of creation,
       cradle of life and the home of our race.

2 Thanks be to God for its bounty and beauty,
       life that sustains us in body and mind;
   plenty for all if we learn how to share it,
       riches un-dreamed of to fathom and find.

3 Long have our human wars ruined its harvest,
       long has earth bowed to the terror of force,
   long have we wasted what others have need of,
       poisoned the fountain of life at its source.

4 Earth is the Lord's: it is ours to enjoy it,
       ours, as his stewards, to farm and defend.
   From its pollution, misuse and damnation
       good Lord, deliver us, world without end.

                                    F Pratt Green

31 God of light and life's creation

BUSHEY HALL

David Iliff

Unison

1 God of light and life's cre - a - tion, reign-ing o - ver all su -
2 God of a - lien, God of stran - ger, named by na-tions of the
3 God of jus - tice in our na - tion, fear-ing nei-ther rich nor
4 God the Fa-ther, Son and Spi - rit, Tri - ni - ty of love and

- preme, daunt - ing our i - ma - gi - na - tion,
earth; poor and ex - ile in a man - ger,
strong, grant - ing truth its vin - di - ca - tion,
grace, through your mer - cy we in - he - rit

pros-pect glo-rious yet un - seen: Lord whom earth and
God of harsh and hum - ble birth: let us all with
pass-ing sen-tence on all wrong: Lord, by whom we
word and wor-ship in this place: let our child-ren

heaven o - bey,   turn   to - wards this   house to - day!
love sin - cere   learn   to wel - come   stran - gers here.
die or live,   hear,   and as you   hear, for - give.
all their days   to   this house re - turn with praise!

1   God of light and life's creation,
     reigning over all supreme,
   daunting our imagination,
     prospect glorious yet unseen:
   Lord whom earth and heaven obey,
     turn towards this house today!

2   God of alien, God of stranger,
     named by nations of the earth;
   poor and exile in a manger,
     God of harsh and humble birth:
   let us all with love sincere
     learn to welcome strangers here.

3   God of justice in our nation,
     fearing neither rich nor strong,
   granting truth its vindication,
     passing sentence on all wrong:
   Lord, by whom we die or live,
     hear, and as you hear, forgive.

4   God the Father, Son and Spirit,
     Trinity of love and grace,
   through your mercy we inherit
     word and worship in this place:
   let our children all their days
     to this house return with praise!

Michael Perry
from 1 Kings 8

32 God of mercy, God of grace

CHRIST, WHOSE GLORY

Malcolm Williamson

1 God of mercy, God of grace,
   show the brightness of your face.
Shine upon us, Saviour, shine,
   fill your church with light divine,
and your saving health extend
   unto earth's remotest end.

2 Let your people praise you, Lord,
   be by all that live adored.
Let the nations shout and sing
   glory to their Saviour King;
let all be, below, above,
   one in joy, and light, and love.

H F Lyte

Music: © 1962 Josef Weinberger Ltd. Reproduced by permission of the copyright owners

33   He comes to us as one unknown

REPTON

C H H Parry

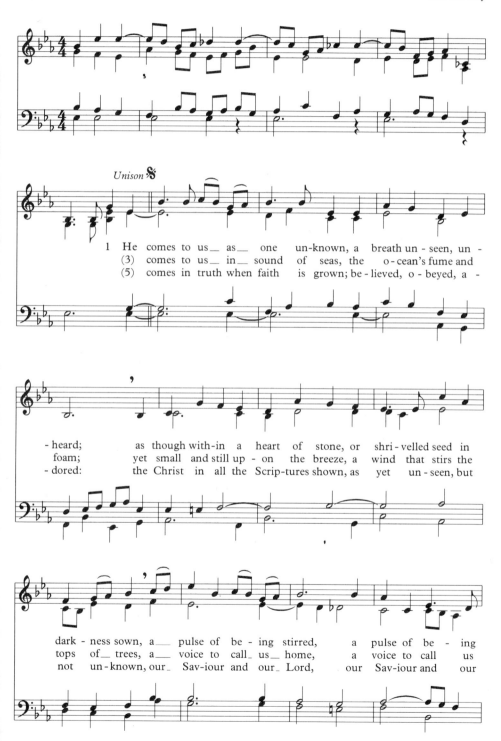

Unison

1 He comes to us as one un-known, a breath un - seen, un -
(3) comes to us in sound of seas, the o - cean's fume and
(5) comes in truth when faith is grown; be - lieved, o - beyed, a -

- heard;   as though with-in a heart of stone, or shri - velled seed in
foam;   yet small and still up - on the breeze, a wind that stirs the
- dored: the Christ in all the Scrip-tures shown, as yet un - seen, but

dark - ness sown, a pulse of be - ing stirred,   a pulse of be - ing
tops of trees, a voice to call us home,   a voice to call us
not un-known, our Sav-iour and our Lord,   our Sav-iour and our

Fine

stirred.
home.
Lord.

2 He comes when souls in__
4 He comes in love as__

si - lence lie and thoughts of day de - part; half -
once he came by flesh and blood and birth; to

- seen up - on the in - ward eye, a fall - ing star a - cross the__ sky of__
bear with - in our mor - tal frame a life, a death, a sav - ing Name, for__

D.S.

night with - in__ the__ heart, of night with - in the heart. 3 He
ev - ery child of__ earth, for ev - ery child of earth. 5 He

1 He comes to us as one unknown,
   a breath unseen, unheard;
as though within a heart of stone,
   or shrivelled seed in darkness sown,
a pulse of being stirred.

2 He comes when souls in silence lie
   and thoughts of day depart;
half-seen upon the inward eye,
   a falling star across the sky
of night within the heart.

3 He comes to us in sound of seas,
   the ocean's fume and foam;
yet small and still upon the breeze,
   a wind that stirs the tops of trees,
a voice to call us home.

4 He comes in love as once he came
   by flesh and blood and birth;
to bear within our mortal frame
   a life, a death, a saving Name,
for every child of earth.

5 He comes in truth when faith is grown;
   believed, obeyed, adored:
the Christ in all the Scriptures shown,
   as yet unseen, but not unknown,
our Saviour and our Lord.

Timothy Dudley-Smith

34 He that is down needs fear no fall

SHEPHERD BOY'S SONG

J H Alden

1 He that is down needs fear no fall, he that is low no pride;

he that is hum-ble ev - er shall have God to be__ his__ guide.

* (Solo or Group)

2 I am con-tent with what I have, lit-tle be it or much;

*This verse is effective as a Treble (or Soprano) solo.

and, Lord, con-tent-ment still I crave, be - cause thou sav - est_ such.

Harmony

3 Full-ness to such a bur-den is that go on pil-grim - age;_

here lit-tle, and here - af - ter bliss, is_ best from age_ to_ age.

1 He that is down needs fear no fall,
   he that is low no pride;
he that is humble ever shall
   have God to be his guide.

2 I am content with what I have,
   little be it or much;
and, Lord, contentment still I crave,
   because thou savest such.

3 Fullness to such a burden is
   that go on pilgrimage;
here little, and hereafter bliss,
   is best from age to age.

John Bunyan

35 I am the Bread

PICKET WOOD

Brian Hoare

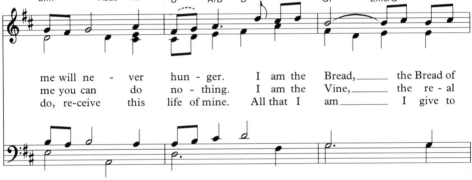

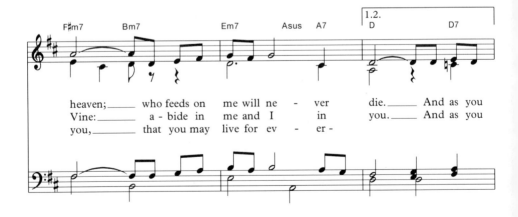

1 I am the Bread,_____ the Bread of Life;_____ who comes to
(2) Vine,_____ the liv-ing Vine;_____ a - part from
(3) bread,_____ and drink this wine,_____ and as you

me will ne - ver hun - ger. I am the Bread,_____ the Bread of
me you can do no - thing. I am the Vine,_____ the re - al
do, re-ceive this life of mine. All that I am_____ I give to

heaven;_____ who feeds on me will ne - ver die._____ And as you
Vine:_____ a - bide in me and I in you. _____ And as you
you,_____ that you may live for ev - er -

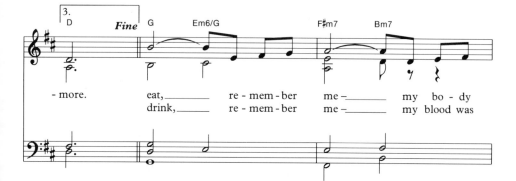

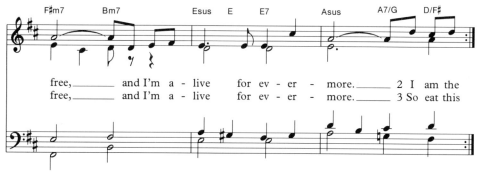

1   I am the Bread, the Bread of Life;
        who comes to me will never hunger.
    I am the Bread, the Bread of heaven;
        who feeds on me will never die.
    And as you eat, remember me –
        my body broken on the tree:
    my life was given to set you free,
        and I'm alive for evermore.

2   I am the Vine, the living Vine;
        apart from me you can do nothing.
    I am the Vine, the real Vine:
        abide in me and I in you.
    And as you drink, remember me –
        my blood was shed upon the tree:
    my life was given to set you free,
        and I'm alive for evermore.

3   So eat this bread, and drink this wine,
        and as you do, receive this life of mine.
    All that I am I give to you,
        that you may live for evermore.

Brian Hoare

36   I come with joy to meet my Lord

FRIENDS

American folk tune
arr Gabriel Jackson

1 I come with joy to meet my Lord, for - giv - en, loved and free,____ in awe and won - der to re - call his life laid down for me,____ his life laid down for me.____

2 I come with Christ - ians far and near to find, as all are fed,____ the new com - mu - ni - ty of love in Christ's com - mun - ion bread,____ in Christ's com - mun - ion bread.____

3 As Christ breaks bread and bids us share, each proud di - vi - sion ends.____ The love that made__ us, makes us one, and stran - gers now__ are friends,____ and stran - gers now__ are friends.____

4 And thus with joy we meet our Lord. His pre - sence, al - ways near,____ is in such friend - ship bet - ter known; we see and praise him here,____ we see and praise him here.____

5 To - ge - ther met, to - ge - ther bound, we'll go our diff - 'rent ways,____ and as his peo - ple in the world, we'll live and speak his praise,____ we'll live and speak his praise.____

1 I come with joy to meet my Lord,
     forgiven, loved and free,
  in awe and wonder to recall
    his life laid down for me,
    his life laid down for me.

2 I come with Christians far and near
    to find, as all are fed,
  the new community of love
    in Christ's communion bread,
    in Christ's communion bread.

3 As Christ breaks bread and bids us share,
    each proud division ends.
  The love that made us, makes us one,
    and strangers now are friends,
    and strangers now are friends.

4 And thus with joy we meet our Lord.
    His presence, always near,
  is in such friendship better known;
    we see and praise him here,
    we see and praise him here.

5 Together met, together bound,
    we'll go our diff'rent ways,
  and as his people in the world,
    we'll live and speak his praise,
    we'll live and speak his praise.

Brian Wren

37   I'll go in the strength of the Lord

IN THE STRENGTH OF THE LORD

Ivor Bosanko

Allegro (♩ = 120)

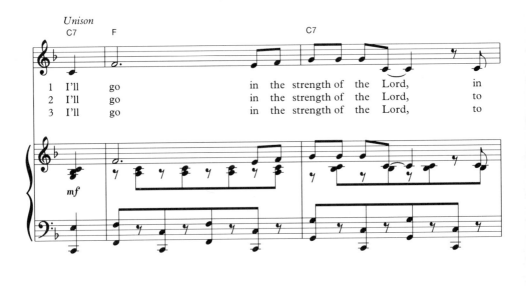

Unison

1   I'll   go   in   the   strength of   the   Lord,   in
2   I'll   go   in   the   strength of   the   Lord,   to
3   I'll   go   in   the   strength of   the   Lord,   to

paths he   has   marked for my   feet;   I'll   fol -   low   the
work he   ap - points   me   to   do;   in   joy   which his
con-flicts which faith   will re - quire,   his   grace   as   my

light of his word, nor shrink from the dan-gers I meet. His
smile doth af-ford_ my soul shall her vi - gour re - new. His
shield and re-ward, my cou-rage and zeal shall in - spire. Since

pre-sence my steps_ shall at - tend, his full-ness my wants shall sup -
wis-dom shall guard_ me from harm, his power my suf-fi - cien-cy
he gives the word_ of com - mand to meet and en-coun - ter the

- ply; on him, till my jour - ney shall end, my un -
prove; I'll trust his om - ni - po-tent arm and_
foe, with his sword of truth_ in my hand, to___

- wa - ver-ing faith shall re - ly:
prove his un-change-ab - le love:
suf - fer and tri - umph I'll go:

Chorus

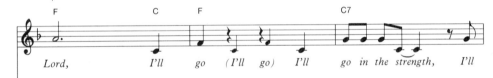

I'll go (I'll go) I'll go in the strength, I'll go in the strength of the

Lord, I'll go (I'll go) I'll go in the strength, I'll

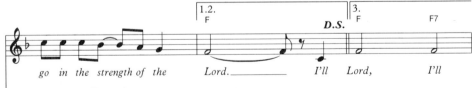

1.2. **3.** **D.S.**

go in the strength of the Lord._____ I'll Lord, I'll

go   in the strength   of the   Lord.

1 I'll go in the strength of the Lord,
       in paths he has marked for my feet;
   I'll follow the light of his word,
       nor shrink from the dangers I meet.
   His presence my steps shall attend,
       his fullness my wants shall supply;
   on him, till my journey shall end,
       my unwavering faith shall rely:

   I'll go (I'll go) in the strength of the Lord,
   I'll go in the strength of the Lord,
   I'll go (I'll go) in the strength of the Lord,
   I'll go in the strength of the Lord.

2 I'll go in the strength of the Lord,
       to work he appoints me to do;
   in joy which his smile doth afford
       my soul shall her vigour renew.
   His wisdom shall guard me from harm,
       his power my sufficiency prove;
   I'll trust his omnipotent arm
       and prove his unchangeable love:
       I'll go (I'll go) . . .

3 I'll go in the strength of the Lord,
       to conflicts which faith will require,
   his grace as my shield and reward,
       my courage and zeal shall inspire.
   Since he gives the word of command
       to meet and encounter the foe,
   with his sword of truth in my hand,
       to suffer and triumph I'll go:
       I'll go (I'll go) . . .

(Repeat last line of Chorus after last verse)

Edward Turney

38 I'll praise the Lord for ever

GREAT CHEVERELL

John Barnard

1 I'll praise the Lord for ev - er and
2 I sought the Lord, he an - swered my
3 O taste and see how gra - cious the
4 The Lord re - deems the faith - ful who

ev - er, my soul shall boast of his won - der - ful name:
call - ing, de - liv - ered me from my in - ner-most fears:
Lord is - se - cure are they who take re - fuge in him:
serve him, and those who trust him he ne - ver con-demns:

Chorus

Glo - ri - fy the Lord with me; ex - alt his name for great is he!
great is he!

I'll

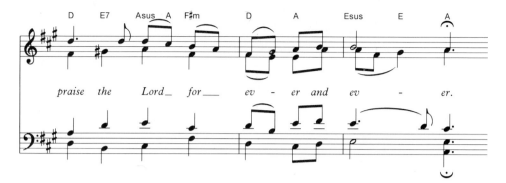

praise the Lord __ for __ ev - er and ev - er.

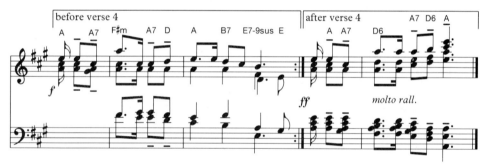

1 I'll praise the Lord for ever and ever,
   my soul shall boast of his wonderful name:

   Glorify the Lord with me;
   exalt his name for great is he!
   I'll praise the Lord for ever and ever.

2 I sought the Lord, he answered my calling,
   delivered me from my innermost fears:
   Glorify the Lord . . .

3 O taste and see how gracious the Lord is –
   secure are they who take refuge in him:
   Glorify the Lord . . .

4 The Lord redeems the faithful who serve him,
   and those who trust him he never condemns:
   Glorify the Lord . . .

Paul Wigmore
from Psalm 34

39 In silent pain the eternal Son

REALITY

John Bell

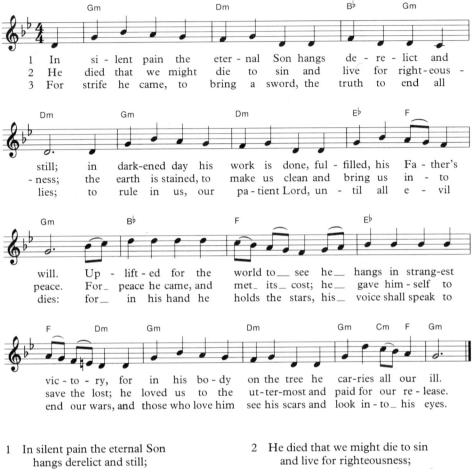

1 In si - lent pain the eter - nal Son hangs de - re - lict and
2 He died that we might die to sin and live for right-eous -
3 For strife he came, to bring a sword, the truth to end all

still; in dark-ened day his work is done, ful - filled, his Fa - ther's
- ness; the earth is stained, to make us clean and bring us in - to
lies; to rule in us, our pa - tient Lord, un - til all e - vil

will. Up - lift - ed for the world to see he hangs in strang-est
peace. For peace he came, and met its cost; he gave him - self to
dies: for in his hand he holds the stars, his voice shall speak to

vic - to - ry, for in his bo - dy on the tree he car - ries all our ill.
save the lost; he loved us to the ut - ter-most and paid for our re - lease.
end our wars, and those who love him see his scars and look in - to his eyes.

1 In silent pain the eternal Son
   hangs derelict and still;
in darkened day his work is done,
   fulfilled, his Father's will.
      Uplifted for the world to see
      he hangs in strangest victory,
      for in his body on the tree
      he carries all our ill.

2 He died that we might die to sin
   and live for righteousness;
the earth is stained, to make us clean
   and bring us into peace.
      For peace he came, and met its cost;
      he gave himself to save the lost;
      he loved us to the uttermost
      and paid for our release.

3 For strife he came, to bring a sword,
   the truth to end all lies;
to rule in us, our patient Lord,
   until all evil dies:
      for in his hand he holds the stars,
      his voice shall speak to end our wars,
      and those who love him see his scars
      and look into his eyes.

Christopher Idle

40 I want Jesus to walk with me

WALK WITH ME

Afro-American traditional Spiritual
arr Lionel Dakers

1 I want Je - sus___ to walk with me,___
(3) trou - ble,___ Lord, walk with me,___

— I want Je - sus___ to walk with me;___
— when I'm in trou - ble,___ Lord, walk with me;___

— all a - long my___ pil - grim jour - ney,___ Lord, I want
— when my head is___ bowed in sor - row,___ Lord, I want

Je - sus___ to walk with me.___ 3 When I'm in

1 I want Jesus to walk with me,
   I want Jesus to walk with me;
      all along my pilgrim journey, Lord,
   I want Jesus to walk with me.

2 In my trials, Lord, walk with me,
   in my trials, Lord, walk with me,
      when my heart is almost breaking, Lord,
   I want Jesus to walk with me.

3 When I'm in trouble, Lord, walk with me,
   when I'm in trouble, Lord, walk with me;
      when my head is bowed in sorrow, Lord,
   I want Jesus to walk with me.

Afro-American traditional

41 I wonder as I wander

I WONDER AS I WANDER

North Carolina Folk song
arranged John J Niles

1 I wonder as I wander, out under the sky,
      how Jesus the Saviour did come for to die
   for poor orn'ry people like you and like I
      I wonder as I wander out under the sky.

2 When Mary birth'd Jesus, 'twas in a cow's stall,
      with wise men and farmers and shepherds and all.
   But high from the heavens a star's light did fall,
      and the promise of ages it then did recall.

3 If Jesus had wanted for any wee thing,
      a star in the sky or a bird on the wing,
   or all of God's angels in heav'n for to sing,
      he surely could have had it, 'cause he was the King.

4 I wonder as I wander out under the sky,
      how Jesus the Saviour did come for to die
   for poor orn'ry people like you and like I
      I wonder as I wander out under the sky.

North Carolina Folk Song
Adapted and transcribed by John J Niles

42 I would be true

LONDONDERRY AIR

Irish traditional
arr Gabriel Jackson

1 I would be true, for there are those who
2 I would be friend of all – the foe, the

trust me:___ I would be pure, for there are those who care;___ I would be
friend-less;___ I would be giv - ing, and for-get the gift;___ I would be

strong, for there is much to suf - fer:___ I would be brave, for there is much to
hum - ble, for I know my weak-ness;_ I would look up, and laugh, and love, and

dare._____ For Christ is true, and he it is who trusts me:___ for Christ is
live._____ He is the friend of all – the foe, the friend-less;_ he is the

pure, and he it is who cares;_____ Je-sus is strong, and he it was who
giv - er who with-holds no gift;_____ and he is hum - ble, show-ing God's own

suf - fered;__ he showed to me ma - jes - tic love__ laid__ bare._____
weak - ness;__ and he looks up, and laughs, and loves and__ lives._____

1   I would be true, for there are those who trust me:
      I would be pure, for there are those who care;
    I would be strong, for there is much to suffer:
      I would be brave, for there is much to dare.
    For Christ is true, and he it is who trusts me:
      for Christ is pure, and he it is who cares;
    Jesus is strong, and he it was who suffered;
      he showed to me majestic love laid bare.

2   I would be friend of all – the foe, the friendless;
      I would be giving, and forget the gift;
    I would be humble, for I know my weakness;
      I would look up, and laugh, and love, and live.
    He is the friend of all – the foe, the friendless;
      he is the giver who withholds no gift;
    and he is humble, showing God's own weakness;
      and he looks up, and laughs, and loves and lives.

H A Walter and J T Wenham

43   Jesus, I know you came

DAFRED

David McCarthy

1 Jesus, I know you came to seek and find me:
2 What if my for-mer self should o-ver-take me?
3 What if an end to doubt is still de-nied me?

yours are the on-ly hands that can un-bind me.
Or new temp-ta-tions wait to bend and break me?
In sac-ra-ment and song you cheer and guide me.

You of-fer me re-lease from sin and sin's in-crease;
You streng-then me to meet my foes up-on my feet;
I have a race to run, each step a vic-tory won;

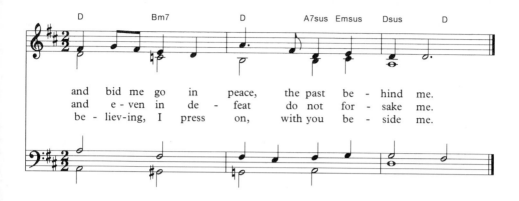

and bid me go in peace, the past be - hind me.
and e - ven in de - feat do not for - sake me.
be - liev-ing, I press on, with you be - side me.

1 Jesus, I know you came
to seek and find me:
yours are the only hands
that can unbind me.
You offer me release
from sin and sin's increase;
and bid me go in peace,
the past behind me.

2 What if my former self
should overtake me?
Or new temptations wait
to bend and break me?
You strengthen me to meet
my foes upon my feet;
and even in defeat
do not forsake me.

3 What if an end to doubt
is still denied me?
In sacrament and song
you cheer and guide me.
I have a race to run,
each step a victory won;
believing, I press on,
with you beside me.

F Pratt Green

44   Jesus the Liberator

THE SPAIN

Cyril Taylor

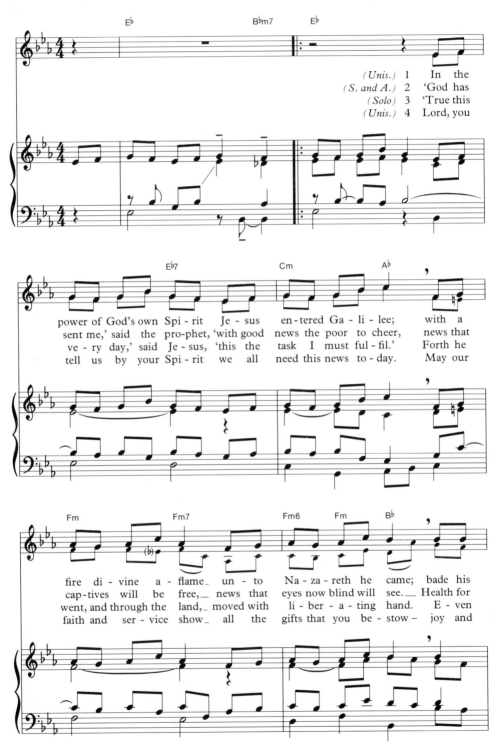

(Unis.) 1 In the power of God's own Spi-rit Je-sus en-tered Ga-li-lee; with a fire di-vine a-flame_ un-to Na-za-reth he came; bade his

(S. and A.) 2 'God has sent me,' said the pro-phet, 'with good news the poor to cheer, news that cap-tives will be free,_ news that eyes now blind will see._ Health for

(Solo) 3 'True this ve-ry day,' said Je-sus, 'this the task I must ful-fil.' Forth he went, and through the land,_ moved with li-ber-a-ting hand.

(Unis.) 4 Lord, you tell us by your Spi-rit we all need this news to-day. May our faith and ser-vice show_ all the gifts that you be-stow_ joy and

1 In the power of God's own Spirit
    Jesus entered Galilee;
with a fire divine aflame
    unto Nazareth he came;
      bade his people hear the scripture:
      'God's anointing Spirit is on me.'

2 'God has sent me,' said the prophet,
    'with good news the poor to cheer,
news that captives will be free,
    news that eyes now blind will see.
      Health for hearts all bruised and broken;
      God's own year of favour now is here.'

3 'True this very day,' said Jesus,
    'this the task I must fulfil.'
Forth he went, and through the land,
    moved with liberating hand.
      Even though men crucified him
      God's unconquered love shone
      through him still.

4 Lord, you tell us by your Spirit
    we all need this news today.
May our faith and service show
    all the gifts that you bestow –
      joy and health and freedom giving,
      Lord, from you, the life, the truth
      the way.

Albert F Bayly
from Luke 4: 14–21

45 Jesus the Lord said

YISU NE KAHA (JESUS SAID)

Urdu traditional melody
arr F B Westbrook

Unison

1 Je - sus the Lord said: 'I am the Bread, the
2 Je - sus the Lord said: 'I am the Door, the
3 Je - sus the Lord said: 'I am the Light, the
4 Je - sus the Lord said: 'I am the Shep-herd, the
5 Je - sus the Lord said: 'I am the Life, the

Bread of___ Life___ for the world am I, the
Way and the Door___ for the poor am I, the
one true___ Light___ of the world am I, the
one Good___ Shep - herd of the sheep am I, the
Re - sur - rec - tion and the Life am I, the

Bread of___ Life___ for the world am I, the
Way and the Door___ for the poor am I, the
one true___ Light___ of the world am I, the
one Good___ Shep - herd of the sheep am I, the
Re - sur - rec - tion and the Life am I, the

Bread of___ Life___ for the world am I.'
Way and the Door___ for the poor am I.'
one true___ Light___ of the world am I.'
one Good___ Shep - herd of the sheep am I.'
Re - sur - rec - tion and the Life am I.'

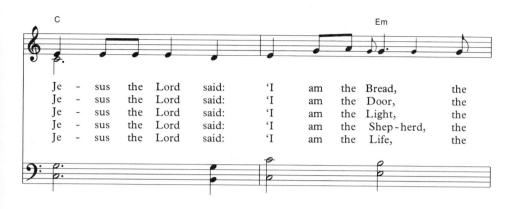

1 Jesus the Lord said: 'I am the Bread,
   the Bread of Life for the world am I,
   the Bread of Life for the world am I,
   the Bread of Life for the world am I.'
   Jesus the Lord said: 'I am the Bread,
   the Bread of Life for the world am I.'

2 Jesus the Lord said: 'I am the Door,
   the Way and the Door for the poor am I.' . . .

3 Jesus the Lord said: 'I am the Light,
   the one true Light of the world am I.' . . .

4 Jesus the Lord said: 'I am the Shepherd,
   the one Good Shepherd of the sheep am I.' . . .

5 Jesus the Lord said: 'I am the Life,
   the Resurrection and the Life am I.' . . .

C D Monahan
Tr from Urdu

46 Jubilate, everybody

JUBILATE, EVERYBODY

F Dunn

Unison

Ju - bi - la - te, ev - ery-bo - dy, serve the Lord in __
all your ways, and come be-fore his pre - sence sing - ing,
en - ter now __ his __ courts with praise. For the Lord our
God is gra - cious, and his mer - cy's ev - er - last - ing.

Ju - bi-la - te,   ju - bi-la - te,   ju - bi-la - te   De - o!

Jubilate, everybody,
    serve the Lord in all your ways,
and come before his presence singing,
    enter now his courts with praise.
For the Lord our God is gracious,
    and his mercy's everlasting.
Jubilate, jubilate,
    jubilate Deo!

F Dunn
from Psalm 100

47 Let us break bread together

BREAD TOGETHER

American Spiritual
arr Charles Cleall

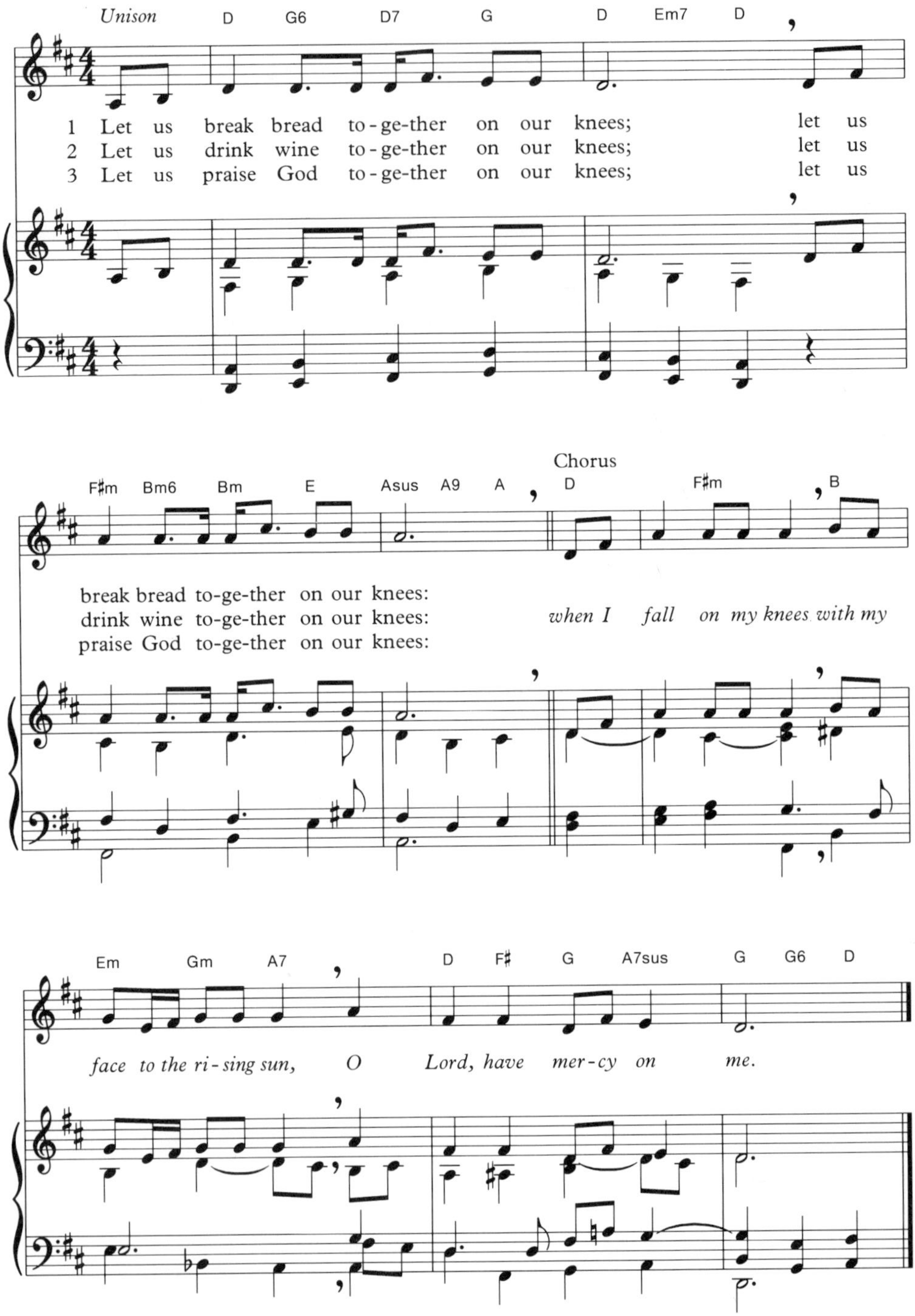

Unison
D G6 D7 G D Em7 D
1 Let us break bread to-ge-ther on our knees; let us
2 Let us drink wine to-ge-ther on our knees; let us
3 Let us praise God to-ge-ther on our knees; let us
F♯m Bm6 Bm E Asus A9 A
break bread to-ge-ther on our knees:
drink wine to-ge-ther on our knees:
praise God to-ge-ther on our knees:
Chorus
D F♯m B
when I fall on my knees with my
Em Gm A7 D F♯ G A7sus G G6 D
face to the ri-sing sun, O Lord, have mer-cy on me.

If guitars are to be used by themselves, the chords used could be:
D Bm Em A | D G D – | F♯m – Bm E | A D A – | F♯m – B – | Em Gm A – | D F♯ G A | D G D – ||

OPTIONAL CHORAL ACCOMPANIMENT FOR VERSE 3

Sopranos sing words of verse 3.   A.T.B. sing vowel 'Oo' or 'Ah'
Use accompaniment on facing page

1 Let us break bread together on our knees;
   let us break bread together on our knees:

     when I fall on my knees
   with my face to the rising sun,
    O Lord, have mercy on me.

2 Let us drink wine together on our knees;
   let us drink wine together on our knees:
     when I fall . . .

3 Let us praise God together on our knees;
   let us praise God together on our knees:
     when I fall . . .

American Spiritual

48   Let us talents and tongues employ

LINSTEAD

Jamaican folk song
arr Doreen Potter

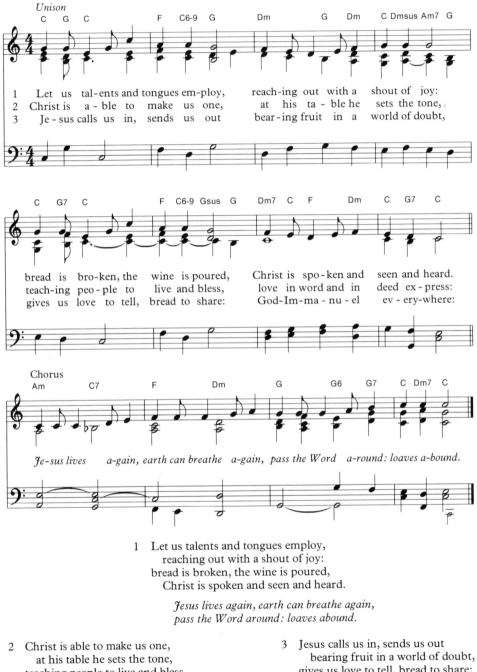

1   Let us talents and tongues employ,
    reaching out with a shout of joy:
    bread is broken, the wine is poured,
    Christ is spoken and seen and heard.

Jesus lives again, earth can breathe again,
pass the Word around: loaves abound.

2   Christ is able to make us one,
    at his table he sets the tone,
    teaching people to live and bless,
    love in word and in deed express:
    Jesus lives again . . .

3   Jesus calls us in, sends us out
    bearing fruit in a world of doubt,
    gives us love to tell, bread to share:
    God-Immanuel everywhere:
    Jesus lives again . . .

Fred Kaan

49 Light of the World

WAVENDON

John Dankworth

Light be-yond sha - dow,

joy be-yond tears, love that is great - er when dark-est our fears;

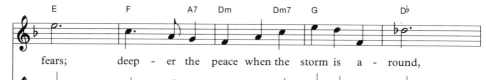

deep - er the peace when the storm is a - round,

2nd time
to Coda ⊕

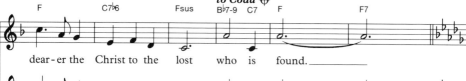

dear-er the Christ to the lost who is found.

Light of the world, Je - sus shin - ing, shin - ing!

Sins of the world, see him dy - ing, dy-ing! In our

dark - ness, he is light, in our

cry - ing, he is love, in the noise of

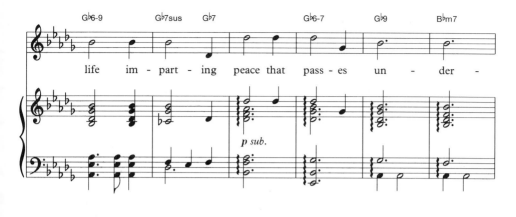

life im-part-ing peace that pass-es un - der -

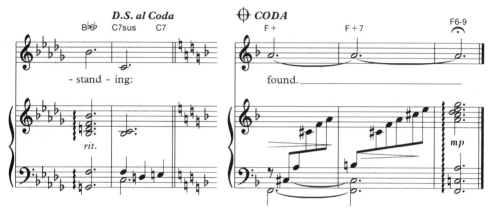

D.S. al Coda

- stand - ing:

⊕ **CODA**

found.

Light beyond shadow, joy beyond tears,
   love that is greater when darkest our fears;
deeper the peace when the storm is around,
   dearer the Christ to the lost who is found.
      Light of the world, Jesus shining, shining!
      Sins of the world, see him dying, dying!
         In our darkness, he is light,
         in our crying, he is love,
         in the noise of life imparting
         peace that passes understanding:
light beyond shadow, joy beyond tears,
   love that is greater when darkest our fears;
deeper the peace when the storm is around,
   dearer the Christ to the lost who is found.

                                    Paul Wigmore

50   Like the murmur of the dove's song

BRIDEGROOM

Peter Cutts

1 Like the mur-mur of the dove's song, like the chal-lenge of her
2 To the mem-bers of Christ's Bo-dy, to the bran-ches of the
3 With the heal-ing of di-vi-sion, with the cease-less voice of

flight, like the vig-our of the wind's rush, like the
Vine, to the Church in faith as-sem-bled, to her
prayer, with the power to love and wit-ness, with the

new flame's ea-ger might: (*All*) come,— Ho-ly Spi-rit, come.
midst as gift and sign: (*All*) come,— Ho-ly Spi-rit, come.
peace be-yond com-pare: (*All*) come,— Ho-ly Spi-rit, come.

A and B may be sung by contrasted groups of voices.

1 Like the murmur of the dove's song,
   like the challenge of her flight,
like the vigour of the wind's rush,
   like the new flame's eager might:
come, Holy Spirit, come.

2 To the members of Christ's Body,
   to the branches of the Vine,
to the Church in faith assembled,
   to her midst as gift and sign:
come, Holy Spirit, come.

3 With the healing of division,
   with the ceaseless voice of prayer,
with the power to love and witness,
   with the peace beyond compare:
come, Holy Spirit, come.

Carl P Daw, Jr

51 Living Lord

LIVING LORD

Patrick Appleford

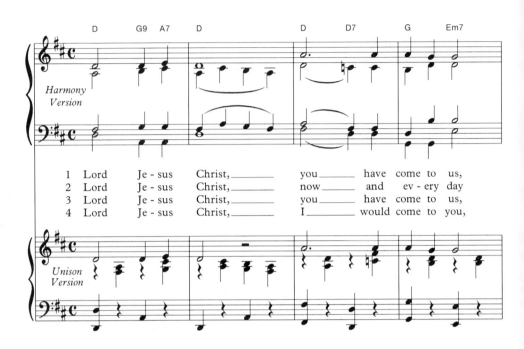

1 Lord Je-sus Christ,_____ you_____ have come to us,
2 Lord Je-sus Christ,_____ now_____ and ev-ery day
3 Lord Je-sus Christ,_____ you_____ have come to us,
4 Lord Je-sus Christ,_____ I_____ would come to you,

Harmony Version

Unison Version

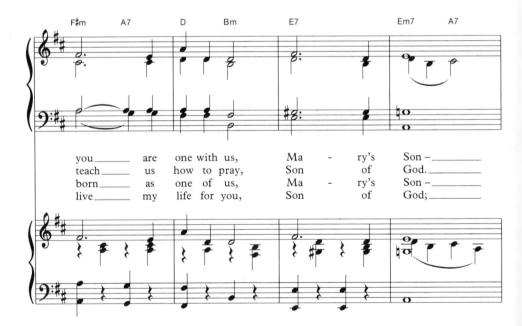

you_____ are one with us, Ma - ry's Son -_____
teach_____ us how to pray, Son of God._____
born_____ as one of us, Ma - ry's Son -_____
live_____ my life for you, Son of God;_____

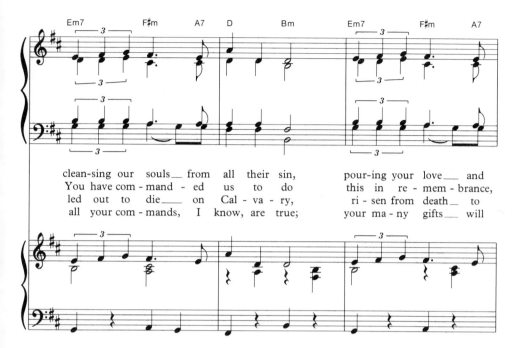

clean-sing our souls__ from all their sin,   pour-ing your love__ and
You have com - mand - ed us to do   this in re - mem - brance,
led out to die__ on Cal - va - ry,   ri - sen from death__ to
all your com - mands, I know, are true;   your ma - ny gifts__ will

good - ness in;   Je - sus, our love for you we sing,
Lord, of you;   in - to our lives your power breaks through,
set us free;   liv - ing Lord Je - sus, help us see
make me new;   in - to my life your power breaks through,

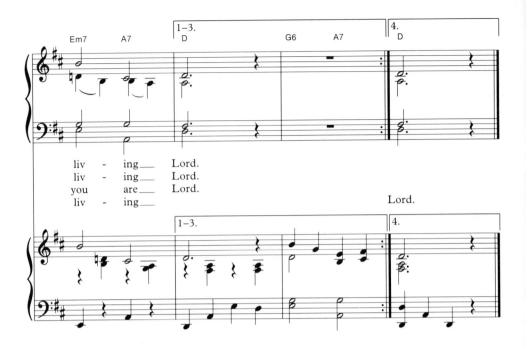

liv - ing___ Lord.
liv - ing___ Lord.
you are___ Lord.
liv - ing___
Lord.

1 Lord Jesus Christ,
   you have come to us,
   you are one with us, Mary's Son –
cleansing our souls from all their sin,
   pouring your love and goodness in;
Jesus, our love for you we sing,
   living Lord.

*2 Lord Jesus Christ,
   now and every day
teach us how to pray, Son of God.
you have commanded us to do
   this, in remembrance, Lord, of you;
into our lives your power breaks through,
   living Lord.

3 Lord Jesus Christ,
   you have come to us,
   born as one of us, Mary's Son –
led out to die on Calvary,
   risen from death to set us free;
living Lord Jesus, help us see
   you are Lord.

4 Lord Jesus Christ,
   I would come to you,
live my life for you, Son of God;
all your commands, I know, are true;
   your many gifts will make me new;
into my life your power breaks through,
   living Lord.

Patrick Appleford

* To be sung only at a Communion service.

Words and music: © 1960 Josef Weinberger Ltd. Reproduced by permission of the copyright owners

52 Lord Jesus, you have promised

HARCOURT TERRACE

Lionel Dakers

1 Lord Je-sus, you have pro-mised to all who fol-low
3 Lord Je-sus Christ, for-give us our sad in-dif-fer-

you that we'll be per-se-cu-ted but you will lead us through. And
-ence; we're not worth per-se-cu-ting, we fear to give of-fence. For-

if we are to serve you we must take up our cross in
-give our lack of glad-ness, for-give our lack of faith; yet

spi-rits will re-joice. Lord Je-sus, you have pro-mised to all who call you friend that you will still be with us till earth-ly time shall end.

1 Lord Jesus, you have promised
    to all who follow you
  that we'll be persecuted
    but you will lead us through.
  And if we are to serve you
    we must take up our cross
  in faithfulness and patience
    through suffering and loss.

2 Lord Jesus, you have promised
    to those who heed your voice
  that through all tribulation
    our spirits will rejoice.
  Lord Jesus, you have promised
    to all who call you friend
  that you will still be with us
    till earthly time shall end.

3 Lord Jesus Christ, forgive us
    our sad indifference;
  we're not worth persecuting,
    we fear to give offence.
  Forgive our lack of gladness,
    forgive our lack of faith;
  yet come to us, renew us,
    lead us to life through death.

John Ferguson

53 Majesty, worship his majesty

MAJESTY

J W Hayford

Maj-es-ty,_____ wor-ship his maj-es-ty;_____ un-to Je-sus be all

hon-our, glo-ry and praise.___ Maj-es-ty,_____ king-dom au-tho-ri-ty_____

___ flow from his throne un-to his own, his an-them raise._____ So ex-

-alt, lift up on high the name of Je - sus;_____ mag-ni - fy, come, glo-ri -

- fy Christ Je-sus the King.   Maj - es - ty,_____ wor-ship his

maj-es-ty;_____ Je-sus who died, now glo-ri - fied, King of all kings._____

*Cued notes optional for a few choir sopranos.

Majesty, worship his majesty;
    unto Jesus be all honour, glory and praise.
Majesty, kingdom authority
    flow from his throne
    unto his own,
    his anthem raise.
So exalt, lift up on high the name of Jesus;
    magnify, come, glorify Christ Jesus the King.
Majesty, worship his majesty;
    Jesus who died,
    now glorified,
    King of all kings.

J W Hayford

54 Make me a channel of your peace

CHANNEL OF PEACE

Melody by Sebastian Temple
arr William Llewellyn

1 Make me a chan-nel of your peace. Where there is hat-red, let me bring your love; where there is in - ju - ry, your par-don, Lord; and when there's doubt, true faith in

2 Make me a chan-nel of your peace. Where there's des-pair in life, let me bring hope; where there is dark-ness, on - ly light; and where there's sad - ness, ev - er

It is in pardon-ing that we are par-doned,— in giv-ing to all men that we re - ceive,— and in dy-ing that we're brought to e-ter-nal life.—

1 Make me a channel of your peace.
    Where there is hatred, let me bring your love;
  where there is injury, your pardon, Lord;
    and when there's doubt, true faith in you:

      O Master, grant that I may never seek
        so much to be consoled as to console;
      to be understood as to understand;
        to be loved as to love with all my soul.

2 Make me a channel of your peace.
    Where there's despair in life, let me bring hope;
  where there is darkness, only light;
    and where there's sadness, ever joy:
      O Master, grant . . .

3 Make me a channel of your peace.
    It is in pardoning that we are pardoned,
  in giving to all men that we receive,
    and in dying that we're brought to eternal life.

Sebastian Temple
from A Prayer of St Francis

55 Make way

MAKE WAY

Graham Kendrick

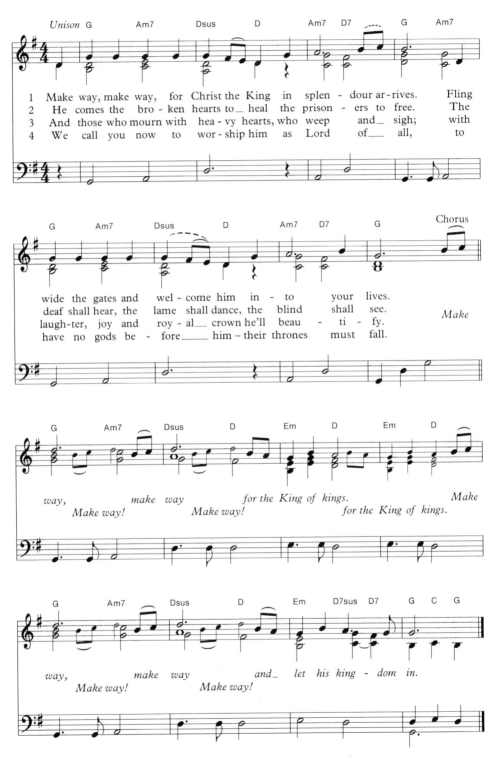

1 Make way, make way, for Christ the King in splen - dour ar-rives. Fling
2 He comes the bro - ken hearts to_ heal the prison - ers to free. The
3 And those who mourn with hea - vy hearts, who weep and_ sigh; with
4 We call you now to wor - ship him as Lord of_ all, to

wide the gates and wel - come him in - to your lives.
deaf shall hear, the lame shall dance, the blind shall see.
laugh-ter, joy and roy - al_ crown he'll beau - ti - fy.
have no gods be - fore_ him – their thrones must fall.

Make

way, *make way* *for the King of kings.* *Make*
Make way! *Make way!* *for the King of kings.*

way, *make way* *and_ let his king - dom in.*
Make way! *Make way!*

1 Make way, make way, for Christ the King
      in splendour arrives.
   Fling wide the gates and welcome him
      into your lives.

      Make way, make way
         for the King of kings.
      Make way, make way
         and let his kingdom in.

2 He comes the broken hearts to heal
      the prisoners to free.
   The deaf shall hear, the lame shall dance,
      the blind shall see.
      Make way . . .

3 And those who mourn with heavy hearts,
      who weep and sigh;
   with laughter, joy and royal crown
      he'll beautify.
      Make way . . .

4 We call you now to worship him
      as Lord of all,
   to have no gods before him –
      their thrones must fall.
      Make way . . .

Graham Kendrick
from Isaiah 40: 3–5; Luke 4: 18–19

56 Morning glory, starlit sky

MORNING GLORY

Barry Rose

1 Morn-ing glo - ry, star-lit sky, soar-ing mu - sic, scho-lar's truth, flight of swal-lows, au-tumn leaves, mem-'ry's trea - sure, grace of youth. 2 O-pen are the gifts of God, gifts of love to mind and sense; hid-den is love's a-go - ny, love's en - dea - vour, love's ex - pense.

3 Love that gives, gives ev - er - more, gives with zeal,＿ with ea - ger

hands, spares not, keeps not, all out - pours, ven-tures all, its all ex -

Tenor Solo

4 Drained is love in mak-ing full, bound in set - ting o-thers

- pends. (*Humming*)

free, poor in keep-ing ma-ny rich, weak in giv - ing power to

be.

p

5 There-fore he who shows us God___ help-less hangs up-on the

1 Morning glory, starlit sky,
   soaring music, scholar's truth,
 flight of swallows, autumn leaves,
   mem'ry's treasure, grace of youth.

2 Open are the gifts of God,
   gifts of love to mind and sense;
 hidden is love's agony,
   love's endeavour, love's expense.

3 Love that gives, gives evermore,
   gives with zeal, with eager hands,
 spares not, keeps not, all outpours,
   ventures all, its all expends.

4 Drained is love in making full,
   bound in setting others free,
 poor in keeping many rich,
   weak in giving power to be.

5 Therefore he who shows us God
   helpless hangs upon the tree;
 and the nails and crown of thorns
   tell of what God's love must be.

6 Here is God, no monarch he,
   throned in easy state to reign;
 here is God, whose arms of love
   aching, spent, the world sustain.

W H Vanstone

CONGREGATIONAL VERSION

1 Morn-ing glo-ry, star-lit sky,___ soar-ing mu - sic, scho-lar's
2 O - pen are the gifts of God,___ gifts of love___ to mind and
3 Love that gives, gives ev - er - more,___ gives with zeal,___ with ea - ger
4 Drained is love in mak-ing full,___ bound in set - ting o - thers
5 There-fore he who shows us God___ help-less hangs___ up - on the
6 Here is God, no mon-arch he,___ throned in ea - sy state to

truth,___ flight of swal - lows, au - tumn leaves,___ mem-'ry's
sense;___ hid - den is love's a - go - ny,___ love's en -
hands,___ spares not, keeps not, all out - pours,___ ven - tures
free,___ poor in keep - ing ma - ny rich,___ weak in
tree;___ and the nails and crown of thorns___ tell of
reign;___ here is God, whose arms of

trea - sure, grace of youth.
- dea - vour, love's ex - pense.
all, its all ex - pends.
giv - ing power to be.
what God's love must be. love___ ach-ing, spent, the world sus - tain.

57 Moses left his palace for love of his people

BURNING BUSH

Cyril Taylor

1 Mo-ses left his pa-lace for love of his peo-ple, gave him-self as torch for the flame of the Word that seared the Red Sea and set free Is-ra-el,

2 Is-ra-el re-ject-ed the word of the Fa-ther, Is-ra-el was blind to the works of his power; and Mo-ses in an-guish lone-ly as E-li-jah;

3 Mo-ses prayed the Fa-ther, for love of his peo-ple, 'Blot me out for ev-er, that Is-rael be re-stored.' In death is God's life, de-feat his vic-to-ry,

4 Je-sus died, re-ject-ed, for love of all peo-ples, died and rose a slave to the will of the Word. He rais-es the dead, re-news God's Is-ra-el,

brought them bread from hea - ven   and   wa - ter from the Lord.
dared   for   them   the   moun-tain,   the   dark-ness   and   the   fire.
bush   his   hand   has   kind - led   can   ne - ver   be   con-sumed.
he   our   bread   from   hea - ven,   our   wa - ter   from   the   rock.

1   Moses left his palace for love of his people,
         gave himself as torch for the flame of the Word
         that seared the Red Sea
         and set free Israel,
     brought them bread from heaven
     and water from the Lord.

2   Israel rejected the word of the Father,
         Israel was blind to the works of his power;
         and Moses in anguish
         lonely as Elijah;
     dared for them the mountain,
     the darkness and the fire.

3   Moses prayed the Father, for love of his people,
         'Blot me out for ever, that Israel be restored.'
         In death is God's life,
         defeat his victory,
     bush his hand has kindled
     can never be consumed.

4   Jesus died, rejected, for love of all peoples,
         died and rose a slave to the will of the Word.
         He raises the dead,
         renews God's Israel,
     he our bread from heaven,
     our water from the rock.

Emily Chisholm

Words: © Revd Dr Leslie Griffiths wih permission (Exor of Emily Chishom).
Music: © 1992 Canterbury Press Norwich.
USA Music: © 1992 by Hope Publishing Company, Carol Stream, IL 60188

58   Now the silence

NOW

Carl F Schalk

Now the si-lence, now the peace, now the emp-ty hands up-lift-ed;

Now the kneel-ing, now the plea, now the Fa-ther's arms in wel-come;

Now the hear-ing, now the power, now the ves-sel brimmed for pour-ing;

Now the Bo-dy, now the Blood, now the joy-ful ce - le-bra-tion;

Now the wed-ding, now the songs, now the heart for-giv - en leap-ing;

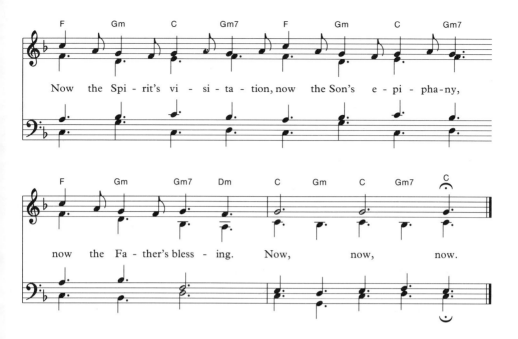

Now the Spi - rit's vi - si - ta - tion, now the Son's e - pi - pha - ny, now the Fa - ther's bless - ing. Now, now, now.

Preparation	Now the silence, now the peace, now the empty hands uplifted;
Confession	Now the kneeling, now the plea,
Absolution	now the Father's arms in welcome;
Sermon	Now the hearing, now the power,
Offertory	now the vessel brimmed for pouring;
Communion	Now the Body, now the Blood, now the joyful celebration;
Union with Christ	Now the wedding, now the songs, now the heart forgiven leaping;
Channels of God's grace	Now the Spirit's visitation, now the Son's epiphany, now the Father's blessing.

Now, now, now.

Jaroslav J Vajda

The song No. 84 entitled 'Then the glory' can be used in conjunction with this song

59 O bless the Lord, O my soul

O BLESS THE LORD

John Bell

O my soul,
Won-der-ful;

O my soul,
Coun-sel-lor;

bless the
Prince of

O bless the Lord,_____ O bless the Lord,_____ O bless the Lord, bless the

His name is Won - der-ful; his name is Coun - sel-lor; his name is Prince of

Lord, and ne - ver for - get his love!
Peace whose King-dom shall have no end.

O my soul,
migh - ty God;

Lord, and ne - ver for - get his love! O bless the Lord,_____ O bless the

Peace whose King-dom shall have no end. He is the migh - ty God; he is the

O my soul,
Lord of Hosts;

bless the Lord and
King of Heaven, our

ne - ver for-get his love!
Sav-iour, our God and Friend.

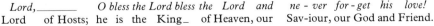

Lord,_____ O bless the Lord bless the Lord and ne - ver for - get his love!

Lord of Hosts; he is the King_ of Heaven, our Sav-iour, our God and Friend.

O bless the Lord, O my soul,
  O bless the Lord, O my soul,
O bless the Lord,
  bless the Lord and never forget his love!
O bless the Lord, O my soul,
  O bless the Lord, O my soul,
O bless the Lord and never forget his love!

His name is Wonderful;
  his name is Counsellor;
his name is Prince of Peace
  whose Kingdom shall have no end.
He is the mighty God;
  he is the Lord of Hosts;
he is the King of Heaven,
  our Saviour, our God and Friend.

John Bell and Graham Maule
adapted from Isaiah 9

This is written for singing in 4-part harmony but it can be sung with half the group taking the bass part and half the top line.

60 O Christ, the healer

TEMPSFORD

Paul Edwards

Unison

1 O Christ, the heal - er, we have come to
2 From ev - ery ail - ment flesh en - dures our
3 How strong, O Lord, are our de - sires, how
4 In con - flicts that des - troy our health we
5 Grant that we all, made one in faith, in

pray for health, to plead for friends. How can we fail to
bo - dies cla - mour to be freed; yet in our hearts we
weak our know - ledge of our-selves! Re - lease in us those
di - ag - nose the world's di - sease: our com - mon life de -
your com - mu - ni - ty may find the whole-ness that, en -

be re - stored, when reached by love that ne - ver ends?
would con - fess that whole-ness is our deep - est need.
heal - ing truths un - con - scious pride re - sists or shelves.
- clares our ills: is there no cure, O Christ, for these?
- rich - ing us, shall reach the whole of hu - man-kind.

1 O Christ, the healer, we have come
    to pray for health, to plead for friends.
How can we fail to be restored,
    when reached by love that never ends?

2 From every ailment flesh endures
    our bodies clamour to be freed;
yet in our hearts we would confess
    that wholeness is our deepest need.

3 How strong, O Lord, are our desires,
    how weak our knowledge of ourselves!
Release in us those healing truths
    unconscious pride resists or shelves.

4 In conflicts that destroy our health
    we diagnose the world's disease:
our common life declares our ills:
    is there no cure, O Christ, for these?

5 Grant that we all, made one in faith,
    in your community may find
the wholeness that, enriching us,
    shall reach the whole of humankind.

F Pratt Green

61 O Lord, my God, you know all my ways

SHEPHERDSWELL

John Barnard

Descant — Ah ... Ah

Unison

1 O___ Lord, my God, you know all my ways, when I
(2 Where) can I go to be far from you? In the
(3 O___) Lord, my God, you cre - a - ted me, in a

sleep and I rise, when I sit or stand; and be -
deep - est of caves, in the heights of heaven? If I
won - der - ful way you have fa-shioned me. Test my

- fore a - ny word is up - on my tongue you dis -
rise up and fly on the wings of dawn still your
spi - rit and see what is in my heart; lead me

- cern it as though I had spo-ken it.
right hand will guide me and hold me fast.
on in the way to e - ter - nal life.

Descant: 3rd time only   Ah

2 Where
3 O___

1   O Lord, my God,
       you know all my ways,
     when I sleep and I rise, when I sit or stand;
     and before any word is upon my tongue
       you discern it as though I had spoken it.

2   Where can I go
       to be far from you?
     In the deepest of caves, in the heights of heaven?
     If I rise up and fly on the wings of dawn
       still your right hand will guide me and hold me fast.

3   O Lord, my God,
       you created me,
     in a wonderful way you have fashioned me.
     Test my spirit and see what is in my heart;
       lead me on in the way to eternal life.

Paul Wigmore
based on Psalm 139

62 O sing a song of Bethlehem

TYROL

Tyrolean melody
arr Gabriel Jackson

1 O sing a song of Beth-le-hem of shep-herds watch-ing there,
2 O sing a song of Na-za-reth, of sun-ny days of joy,
3 O sing a song of Ga-li-lee, of lake and woods and hill,
4 O sing a song of Cal-va-ry, its glo-ry and dis-may;

and of the news that came to__ them from an-gels in the air:
O sing of fra-grant flo-wers' breath and of the sin-less boy;
of him who walked up-on the__ sea and bade its waves be still:
of him who hung up-on the__ tree, and took our sins a-way:

the light that shone on Beth-le-hem fills all the world to-day;
for now the flowers of Na-za-reth in ev-ery heart may grow;
for though, like waves on Ga-li-lee, dark seas of trou-ble roll,
for he who died on Cal-va-ry is ris-en from the grave,

of   Je - sus' birth and   peace on__ earth the   an - gels sing   al - way.
now   spreads the fame of   his   dear name on   all   the winds that   blow.
when faith   has heard the   Mas - ter's word falls   peace up - on   the   soul.
and   Christ our Lord, by   heaven a - dored, is   migh - ty now   to   save.

1 O sing a song of Bethlehem
      of shepherds watching there,
   and of the news that came to them
      from angels in the air:
   the light that shone on Bethlehem
      fills all the world today;
   of Jesus' birth and peace on earth
      the angels sing alway.

2 O sing a song of Nazareth,
      of sunny days of joy,
   O sing of fragrant flowers' breath
      and of the sinless boy;
   for now the flowers of Nazareth
      in every heart may grow;
   now spreads the fame of his dear name
      on all the winds that blow.

3 O sing a song of Galilee,
      of lake and woods and hill,
   of him who walked upon the sea
      and bade its waves be still:
   for though, like waves on Galilee,
      dark seas of trouble roll,
   when faith has heard the Master's word
      falls peace upon the soul.

4 O sing a song of Calvary,
      its glory and dismay;
   of him who hung upon the tree,
      and took our sins away:
   for he who died on Calvary
      is risen from the grave,
   and Christ our Lord, by heaven adored,
      is mighty now to save.

Louis F Benson

63　O gracious Light

THE EIGHTH TUNE

Thomas Tallis, adapted

This may be sung unaccompanied as a four-part canon.

1 O gracious Light, Lord Jesus Christ,
　　in you the Father's glory shone.
　Immortal, holy, blest is he,
　　and blest are you, his holy Son.

2 Now sunset comes, but light shines forth,
　　the lamps are lit to pierce the night.
　Praise Father, Son and Spirit; God
　　who dwells in the eternal light.

3　Worthy are you of endless praise,
　　　O Son of God, life-giving Lord;
　　wherefore you are through all the earth
　　　and in the highest heaven adored.

3rd-century Greek
tr F Bland Tucker

64   One more step along the world

SOUTHCOTE

Sydney Carter
arr Lionel Dakers

1 One more step a - long the
3 As I tra - vel through the
5 You are old - er than the

world I go,   one more step a - long the world I go;
bad and good,   keep me tra - vel - ling the way I should;
world can be,   you are young - er than the life in me;

from the old things to the new   keep me tra - vel - ling a -
where I see no way to go   you'll be tell - ing me the
ev - er old and ev - er new,   keep me tra - vel - ling a -

- long   with   you.
way,   I   know: *And it's from*   *the*   *old*   *I*
- long   with   you:

tra-vel to the new;   *keep*   *me tra-vel-ling a-long with you.*

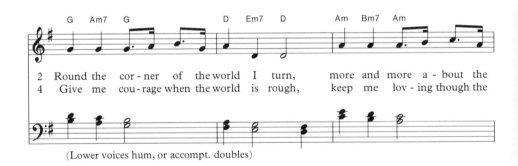

2   Round the   cor-ner   of   the world   I   turn,   more   and   more   a-bout   the
4   Give me   cou-rage when the world   is   rough,   keep   me   lov-ing though the

(Lower voices hum, or accompt. doubles)

world   I   learn;   all   the   new   things   that   I   see
world   is   tough;   leap   and   sing   in   all   I   do,

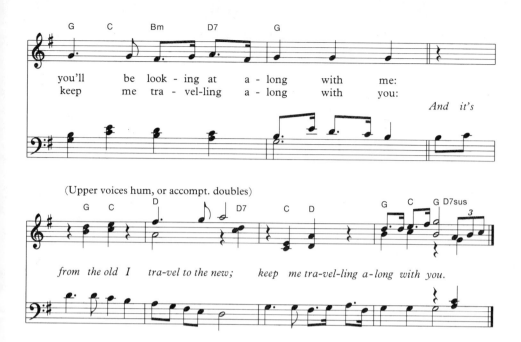

(Upper voices hum, or accompt. doubles)

from the old I tra-vel to the new; keep me tra-vel-ling a-long with you.

1 One more step along the world I go,
 one more step along the world I go;
from the old things to the new
 keep me travelling along with you.

 And it's from the old I travel to the new;
 keep me travelling along with you.

2 Round the corner of the world I turn,
 more and more about the world I learn;
all the new things that I see
 you'll be looking at along with me:
 And it's from the old . . .

3 As I travel through the bad and good,
 keep me travelling the way I should;
where I see no way to go
 you'll be telling me the way, I know:
 And it's from the old . . .

4 Give me courage when the world is rough,
 keep me loving though the world is tough;
leap and sing in all I do,
 keep me travelling along with you:
 And it's from the old . . .

5 You are older than the world can be,
 you are younger than the life in me;
ever old and ever new,
 keep me travelling along with you:
 And it's from the old . . .

Sydney Carter

65 Reach out and touch the Lord

Bill Harmon

1 Reach out and touch the Lord___ as he___ goes
2 Look___ up and see the Lord___ as he___ goes
3 Be___ still and hear the Lord___ as he___ goes

by; you'll find he's not too bu - sy to___ hear your heart's
by; you'll see the light of mer - cy and___ love in his
by; you'll hear the sweet-est mu - sic of___ heav'n in his

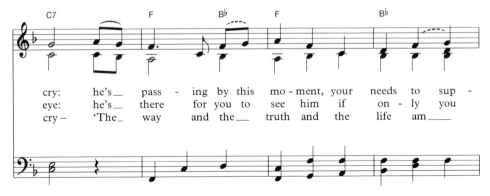

cry: he's___ pass - ing by this mo - ment, your needs to sup -
eye: he's___ there for you to see him if on - ly you
cry – 'The___ way and the___ truth and the life am___

- ply – reach out and touch the Lord___ as___ he goes by.
try – look up and see the Lord___ as___ he goes by.
I!' Be still and hear the Lord___ as___ he goes by.

1   Reach out and touch the Lord as he goes by;
        you'll find he's not too busy to hear your heart's cry:
    he's passing by this moment, your needs to supply –
    reach out and touch the Lord as he goes by.

2   Look up and see the Lord as he goes by;
        you'll see the light of mercy and love in his eye:
    he's there for you to see him if only you try –
    look up and see the Lord as he goes by.

3   Be still and hear the Lord as he goes by;
        you'll hear the sweetest music of heav'n in his cry –
    'The way and the truth and the life am I!'
    Be still and hear the Lord as he goes by.

Bill Harmon verse 1
Paul Wigmore verses 2 and 3

66 Rejoice in the Lord

Evelyn Tarner

Words and music: Reproduced from *50 Sacred Canons and Rounds* (Ed. Kenneth Simpson) By permission of Novello & Company Limited

67 Sent forth by God's blessing

THE ASH GROVE

arr Lionel Dakers

1 Sent forth by God's bless-ing, our
2 With praise and thanks-giv - ing to

true faith con - fess-ing, the peo-ple of_ God from his dwell-ing take leave.
God ev - er_ liv-ing, the tasks of_ our ev - ery-day life we will face,

*The sup-per is_ end-ed: O_ now be_ ex - tend-ed the_
our faith ev - er_ shar-ing, in_ love ev - er_ car - ing, re -

*This section in 4-part harmony, either unaccompanied or accompaniment doubling voice parts.

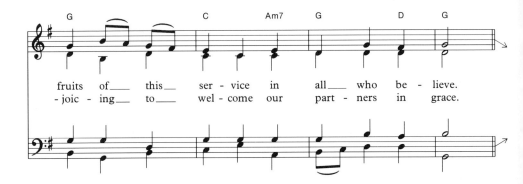

fruits of___ this__ ser - vice in all__ who be - lieve.
-joic - ing__ to__ wel - come our part - ners in grace.

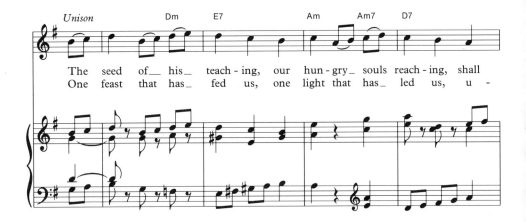

The seed of__ his_ teach - ing, our hun - gry_ souls reach - ing, shall
One feast that has_ fed us, one light that has_ led us, u -

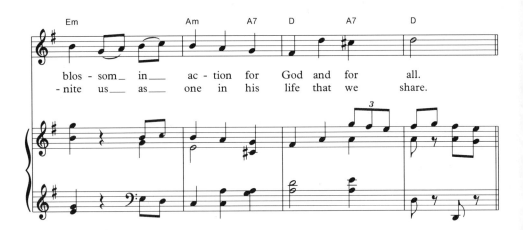

blos - som_ in__ ac - tion for God and for all.
-nite us__ as__ one in his life that we share.

1 Sent forth by God's blessing, our true faith confessing,
    the people of God from his dwelling take leave.
The supper is ended: O now be extended
    the fruits of this service in all who believe.
The seed of his teaching, our hungry souls reaching,
    shall blossom in action for God and for all.
His grace did invite us, his love shall unite us
    to work for his kingdom and answer his call.

2 With praise and thanksgiving to God ever living,
    the tasks of our everyday life we will face,
our faith ever sharing, in love ever caring,
    rejoicing to welcome our partners in grace.
One feast that has fed us, one light that has led us,
    unite us as one in his life that we share.
Then may all the living, with praise and thanksgiving,
    give honour to Christ and his name that we bear.

Omer Westendorff

68 Safe in the shadow of the Lord

STANTON

John Barnard

Unison

1 Safe in the sha - dow of the Lord, be - neath his
2 My hope is set on God a - lone, though Sa - tan
3 From fears and phan - toms of the night, from foes a -
4 His ho - ly an - gels keep my feet se - cure from
5 Strong in the ev - er - last - ing name, and in my
6 Safe in the sha - dow of the Lord, pos - sessed by

hand_ and power, I trust in him, I trust in
spreads his snare; I trust in him, I trust in
- bout_ my way, I trust in him, I trust in
ev - ery stone; I trust in him, I trust in
Fa - ther's care, I trust in him, I trust in
love_ di - vine, I trust in him, I trust in

him, my for - tress and_ my tower.
him, to keep me in_ his care.
him, by dark - ness as_ by day.
him, and un - a - fraid_ go on.
him, who hears and ans - wers prayer.
him, and meet his love_ with mine.

This arrangement is suitable for all keyboard instruments. The accompaniment opposite is specifically for organ

ORGAN ACCOMPANIMENT

4-PART HARMONY

Ah

Ah

1 Safe in the shadow of the Lord,
   beneath his hand and power,
  I trust in him, I trust in him,
   my fortress and my tower.

2 My hope is set on God alone,
   though Satan spreads his snare;
  I trust in him, I trust in him,
   to keep me in his care.

3 From fears and phantoms of the night,
   from foes about my way,
  I trust in him, I trust in him,
   by darkness as by day.

4 His holy angels keep my feet
   secure from every stone;
  I trust in him, I trust in him,
   and unafraid go on.

5 Strong in the everlasting name,
   and in my Father's care,
  I trust in him, I trust in him,
   who hears and answers prayer.

6 Safe in the shadow of the Lord,
   possessed by love divine,
  I trust in him, I trust in him,
   and meet his love with mine.

Timothy Dudley-Smith
from Psalm 91

69 See him lying on a bed of straw

CALYPSO CAROL

Michael Perry
arr Stephen Coates

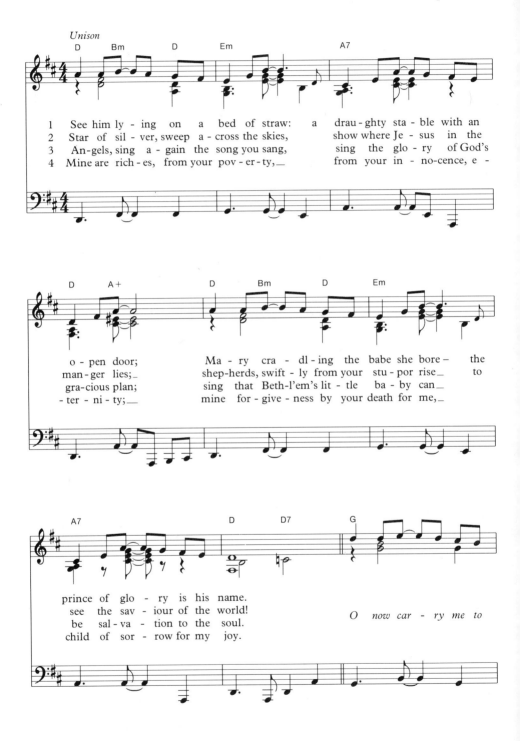

1 See him ly - ing on a bed of straw: a drau - ghty sta - ble with an
2 Star of sil - ver, sweep a - cross the skies, show where Je - sus in the
3 An - gels, sing a - gain the song you sang, sing the glo - ry of God's
4 Mine are rich - es, from your pov - er - ty,— from your in - no - cence, e -

o - pen door; Ma - ry cra - dl - ing the babe she bore – the
man - ger lies;— shep - herds, swift - ly from your stu - por rise_ to
gra - cious plan; sing that Beth-l'em's lit - tle ba - by can_ be
- ter - ni - ty;— mine for - give - ness by your death for me,— child

prince of glo - ry is his name.
see the sav - iour of the world!
be sal - va - tion to the soul.
child of sor - row for my joy.

O now car - ry me to

Beth-le-hem to see the Lord's pure love a-gain: just as poor as was the

sta - ble then, the prince of glo - ry when he came.

1 See him lying on a bed of straw:
    a draughty stable with an open door;
  Mary cradling the babe she bore –
    the prince of glory is his name.

  O now carry me to Bethlehem
    to see the Lord's pure love again:
  just as poor as was the stable then,
    the prince of glory when he came.

2 Star of silver, sweep across the skies,
    show where Jesus in the manger lies;
  shepherds, swiftly from your stupor rise
    to see the saviour of the world!
    O now carry me . . .

3 Angels, sing again the song you sang,
    sing the glory of God's gracious plan;
  sing that Bethl'em's little baby can
    be salvation to the soul.
    O now carry me . . .

4 Mine are riches, from your poverty,
    from your innocence, eternity;
  mine forgiveness by your death for me,
    child of sorrow for my joy.
    O now carry me . . .

Michael Perry

70 Seek ye first

Karen Lafferty

Rich and broad

1 Seek ye___ first the___ king - dom of God
2 Ask, and___ it shall___ be given un - to you,
3 Man shall not live by___ bread___ a - lone,

and his___ right - eous - ness; and all these things shall be
seek, and___ ye shall find; knock, and the door shall be
but by___ ev - ery___ word that pro - ceeds from the

add - ed un - to you; Al - le - lu, al - le - lu - ia.
o-pened un-to you; Al - le - lu, al - le - lu - ia.
mouth of the Lord; Al - le - lu, al - le - lu - ia.

Al - le - lu - ia, al - le -

Seek ye___ first the___ king - dom of God and his right - eous -
Ask, and___ it shall be given un - to you, seek, and___ ye shall
Man shall not live by___ bread a - lone, but by___ ev - ery___

1 Seek ye first the kingdom of God
  and his righteousness;
  and all these things shall be added unto you;
  alleluia.

2 Ask, and it shall be given unto you,
  seek, and ye shall find;
  knock, and the door shall be opened unto you;
  alleluia.

3 Man shall not live by bread alone,
  but by every word
  that proceeds from the mouth of the Lord;
  alleluia.

Karen Lafferty

71 Shine, Jesus, Shine

SHINE, JESUS, SHINE

Graham Kendrick

Unison

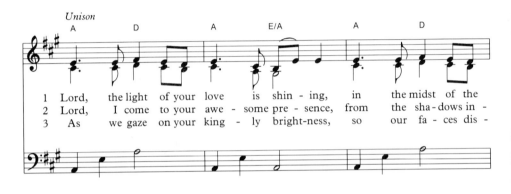

1 Lord, the light of your love is shin - ing, in the midst of the
2 Lord, I come to your awe - some pre - sence, from the sha - dows in -
3 As we gaze on your king - ly bright-ness, so our fa - ces dis -

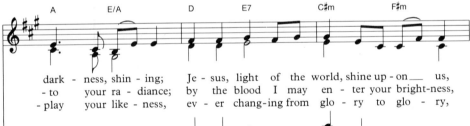

dark - ness, shin - ing; Je - sus, light of the world, shine up - on __ us,
- to your ra - diance; by the blood I may en - ter your bright-ness,
- play your like - ness, ev - er chang-ing from glo - ry to glo - ry,

set us free by the truth you now bring us, shine on __ me,
search me, try me, con-sume all my dark-ness: shine on __ me,
mir-rored here, may our lives tell your sto - ry: shine on __ me,

shine on___ me: *Shine, Je-sus, shine,* ___ *fill this*

land with the Fa-ther's glo-ry; blaze, Spi-rit, blaze, ___ *set our*

hearts on fire. Flow, ri-ver, flow, ___ *flood the*

na-tions with love and mer-cy; send forth your word, ___ *Lord, and*

let there be light!

1 Lord, the light of your love is shining,
      in the midst of the darkness, shining;
   Jesus, light of the world, shine upon us,
      set us free by the truth you now bring us,
      shine on me, shine on me.

      Shine, Jesus, shine,
         fill this land with the Father's glory;
      blaze, Spirit, blaze,
         set our hearts on fire.
      Flow, river, flow,
         flood the nations with love and mercy;
         send forth your word, Lord, and let there be light!

2 Lord, I come to your awesome presence,
      from the shadows into your radiance;
   by the blood I may enter your brightness,
      search me, try me, consume all my darkness:
      shine on me, shine on me:
      Shine, Jesus, shine . . .

3 As we gaze on your kingly brightness,
      so our faces display your likeness,
   ever changing from glory to glory,
      mirrored here, may our lives tell your story:
      shine on me, shine on me:
      Shine, Jesus, shine . . .

                                    Graham Kendrick
                                    from John 12: 46

72 Show me your hands

HERONPARK

Nigel Don

Show me your hands, your hands that woke the dead,
    your hands that broke the bread
    and poured the wine;
through faith I'll see your healing hands on mine,
    then I shall feel
    your power to save and heal.

Paul Wigmore

73 Sing a new song to the Lord

ONSLOW SQUARE

David G Wilson

1 Sing   a new song to the Lord,   he   to whom won-ders be -
2 Now   to the ends of the earth   see   his sal - va - tion is
3 Sing   a new song and re - joice,   pub - lish his prais - es a -
4 Join   with the hills and the   sea   thun - ders of praise to pro -

- long;_____ re - joice_____ in his tri - umph__ and
shown;_____ and still_____ he re - mem - bers____ his
- broad;_____ let voic - es in cho - rus,_____ with
- long;_____ in judge - ment and jus - tice_____ he

tell_____ of his power –_____ O sing_____ to the
mer - cy and truth,_____ un - chang - ing in
trum - pet and horn,_____ re - sound_____ for the
comes_____ to the earth –_____ O sing_____ to the

Lord_____ a new song!
love_____ to his own.
joy_____ of the Lord!
Lord_____ a new song!

1 Sing a new song to the Lord,
   he to whom wonders belong;
   rejoice in his triumph and tell of his power –
   O sing to the Lord a new song!

2 Now to the ends of the earth
   see his salvation is shown;
   and still he remembers his mercy and truth,
   unchanging in love to his own.

3 Sing a new song and rejoice,
   publish his praises abroad;
   let voices in chorus, with trumpet and horn,
   resound for the joy of the Lord!

4 Join with the hills and the sea
   thunders of praise to prolong;
   in judgement and justice he comes to the earth –
   O sing to the Lord a new song!

Timothy Dudley-Smith

74   Sing, sing, sing to the Lord

BOW COMMON LANE

Stephen James

1 Sing, sing,
2 Great, great,
3 Bring, bring,
4 Joy, joy,

sing   to the   Lord,   sing,   ev - ery   land,   your   own   new
great   is the   Lord,   great   and most   wor - thy   of   our
bring   to the   Lord,   bring   to his   name   the   wor - ship
joy   in the   heavens,   joy   for the   life   of   sea   and

song;   sing   of your   Sav-iour each   day!_____
love,   great   a - bove   all   o - ther   gods:_____
due,   bring   your best   gift   to   his   throne:_____
earth,   joy   in the   field and the   wood!_____

Let   all   the   na - tions   hear   of his   glo - ry,   vic - tor - ies,
they   are   but   no - thing,   God   is all -   glo-rious,   splen-did, ma -
God   is   all -   ho - ly,   trem - ble be - fore him,   clothed in   his
Wel-come   his   king-dom,   praise   his sal -   va-tion;   now   he   is

won-ders, tell them the sto - ry — prais-ing the Lord with
- jes - tic, strong and vic - tor-ious, ma - ker of earth and
beau - ty, come to a - dore him — tell what the Lord has
com - ing, Lord of cre - a - tion, judg-ing the peo - ples

heart and tongue, prais-ing the Lord with heart and tongue.
heaven a - bove, ma - ker of earth and heaven a - bove.
done for you, tell what the Lord has done for you.
with his truth, judg-ing the peo - ples with his truth.

1 Sing, sing, sing to the Lord,
      sing, every land, your own new song;
   sing of your Saviour each day!
         Let all the nations hear of his glory,
            victories, wonders, tell them the story –
      praising the Lord with heart and tongue,
      praising the Lord with heart and tongue.

2 Great, great, great is the Lord,
      great and most worthy of our love,
   great above all other gods:
         they are but nothing, God is all-glorious,
            splendid, majestic, strong and victorious,
      maker of earth and heaven above,
      maker of earth and heaven above.

3 Bring, bring, bring to the Lord,
      bring to his name the worship due,
   bring your best gift to his throne:
         God is all-holy, tremble before him,
            clothed in his beauty, come to adore him –
      tell what the Lord has done for you,
      tell what the Lord has done for you.

4 Joy, joy, joy in the heavens,
      joy for the life of sea and earth,
   joy in the field and the wood!
         Welcome his kingdom, praise his salvation;
            now he is coming, Lord of creation,
      judging the peoples with his truth,
      judging the peoples with his truth.

Christopher Idle
from Psalm 96

75   Spirit of faith, by faith be mine

LITTLE STANMORE

John Barnard

1 Spi-rit of faith, by faith be mine;__ Spi-rit of truth, in wis-dom shine;

2 Come to our hearts and there re-main;__ Spi-rit of life,__ our life__ sus-tain;__

Spi - rit of ho - li - ness di - vine,_ Spi - rit of Je - sus,_
Spi - rit of grace_ and glo - ry, reign! Spi - rit of Je - sus,_

come!

come!

1   Spirit of faith, by faith be mine;
        Spirit of truth, in wisdom shine;
    Spirit of holiness divine,
        Spirit of Jesus, come!

2   Come to our hearts and there remain;
        Spirit of life, our life sustain;
    Spirit of grace and glory, reign!
        Spirit of Jesus, come!

Timothy Dudley-Smith

76 Spirit of holiness

BLOW THE WIND SOUTHERLY

Traditional
arr Lionel Dakers

Spi-rit of

ho - li - ness, wis - dom and faith - ful - ness, wind of the Lord, blow - ing

strong-ly and free: strength of our serv-ing and joy of our

wor - ship - ping — Spi - rit of God, bring your full - ness to me!

Spirit of holiness, wisdom and faithfulness,
wind of the Lord, blowing strongly and free:
strength of our serving and joy of our worshipping –
Spirit of God, bring your fullness to me!

1   You came to interpret and teach us effectively
    all that the Saviour has spoken and done;
    to glorify Jesus is all your activity –
    promise and gift of the Father and Son:
       Spirit of holiness . . .

2   You came with your gifts to supply all our poverty,
    pouring your love on the church in her need;
    you came with your fruit for our growth to maturity,
    richly refreshing the souls that you feed:
       Spirit of holiness . . .

Christopher Idle

77 Sing of the Lord's goodness

Ernest Sands
arr Paul Inwood

1 Sing of the Lord's good-ness,
2 Pow - er he has wield - ed,
3 Cour - age in our dark-ness,
4 Praise him with your sing - ing,

Fa - ther of all wis - dom, come to him and bless his
hon - our is his gar - ment, ris - en from the snares of
com - fort in our sor - row, Spi - rit of our God most
praise him with the trum - pet, praise God with the lute and

name._____ Mer - cy he has shown us, his love is for ev - er,
death._____ His word he has spo - ken, one bread he has bro - ken,
high;_____ sol - ace for the wea - ry, par - don for the sin - ner,
harp;_____ praise him with the cym - bals, praise him with your danc - ing,

faith - ful   to the end of   days:_____
new   life he now gives to   all:_____
splen-dour of the liv - ing God:_____
praise God till the end of   days:_____

Chorus

Come, then, all you na-tions,

sing of your Lord's good-ness,   me - lo - dies of praise and   thanks   to   God.

Ring out the Lord's glo - ry,   praise him with your mu - sic,   wor-ship him and bless his

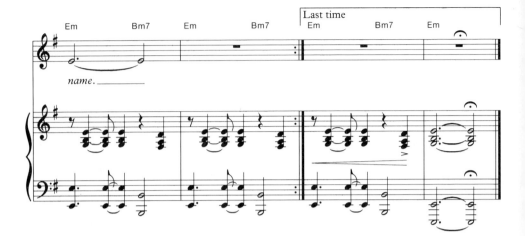

name.

1 Sing of the Lord's goodness, Father of all wisdom,
   come to him and bless his name.
   Mercy he has shown us, his love is for ever,
   faithful to the end of days:

   Come, then, all you nations,
   sing of your Lord's goodness,
   melodies of praise and thanks to God.
   Ring out the Lord's glory,
   praise him with your music,
   worship him and bless his name.

2 Power he has wielded, honour is his garment,
   risen from the snares of death.
   His word he has spoken, one bread he has broken,
   new life he now gives to all:
   Come, then, all . . .

3 Courage in our darkness, comfort in our sorrow,
   Spirit of our God most high;
   solace for the weary, pardon for the sinner,
   splendour of the living God:
   Come, then, all . . .

4 Praise him with your singing, praise him with the trumpet,
   praise God with the lute and harp;
   praise him with the cymbals, praise him with your dancing,
   praise God till the end of days:
   Come, then, all . . .

                                        Ernest Sands

78 Spirit of the living God

SPIRIT OF THE LIVING GOD

Unknown
arr David Iliff

Spirit of the living God, fall afresh on me!
Spirit of the living God, fall afresh on me.
Melt me! Mould me! Fill me! Use me!
Spirit of the living God, fall afresh on me.

Daniel Iverson
from Philippians 3: 21

79 The Bread of Life

GOD'S GRACE

Su Yin-Lan

1 The Bread of Life, for all men bro - ken –
2 With god - ly fear we seek your pre - sence;
3 O Lord, we pray, come now a - mong us,

he drank the cup on Gol - go - tha.
our hearts are sad, peo - ple dis - tressed.
light - en our eyes, bright - ly ap - pear;

His grace we trust, and spread with re - ve - rence
Your ho - ly face is stained with bit - ter tears,
Im - ma - nu - el, heaven's joy un - end - ing,

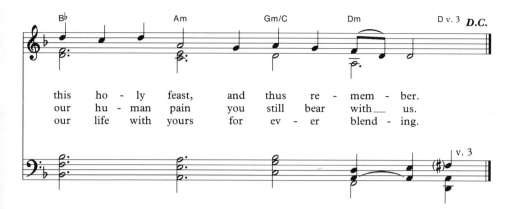

this ho - ly feast, and thus re - mem - ber.
our hu - man pain you still bear with___ us.
our life with yours for ev - er blend - ing.

1 The Bread of Life, for all men broken –
   he drank the cup on Golgotha.
   His grace we trust, and spread with reverence
   this holy feast, and thus remember.

2 With godly fear we seek your presence;
   our hearts are sad, people distressed.
   Your holy face is stained with bitter tears,
   our human pain you still bear with us.

3 O Lord, we pray, come now among us,
   lighten our eyes, brightly appear;
   Immanuel, heaven's joy unending,
   our life with yours for ever blending.

Timothy Tingfang Lew
tr W R O Taylor

80 The Family Table

LAND OF REST

American folk hymn melody
arr John Wilson

1 Be known to us in break-ing bread, but do_ not then de - part;___ Sa - viour, a - bide_ with us,_ and_ spread thy_ ta - ble in_ our heart.___

2 There sup with us_ in

*Verse 1 may be sung by a soloist or small group, with optional humming accompaniment.

love_ di-vine, thy bo - dy and_ thy blood;_____ that liv - ing bread, that

heaven - ly__ wine,_ be__ our__ im - mor - tal food._____

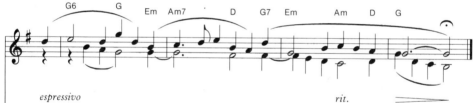

espressivo   *rit.*

1   Be known to us in breaking bread,
       but do not then depart;
    Saviour, abide with us, and spread
       thy table in our heart.

2   There sup with us in love divine,
       thy body and thy blood;
    that living bread, that heavenly wine,
       be our immortal food.

James Montgomery

81 The hands of Christ

MEDFIELD STREET

Simon Beckley
arr John Barnard

Unison

(optional bass)

1 The hands of Christ, the car - ing hands, they nailed them to a
2 The king - ly Christ, the sav - iour-king, they ringed his head with
3 Too late for life, in death too late they tried to maim him
4 To him be praise, all praise to him who died up - on the

cross of wood; the feet that climbed the de - sert road_ and
briars wo - ven;_ the lips that free - ly spoke of heaven, that
with a spear; for sac - ri - lege they could not bear – the
cross of pain; whose a - go - nies were not in vain – for

brought the news of peace with God, they pierced them through.
told the world of sins for - given, they mocked with wine.
sab - bath comes, so they must tear the heart from God.
Christ the Lord is risen a - gain and brings us joy!

This melody is particularly effective when sung unaccompanied. Pianists are recommended to make sparing use of the optional bass, perhaps only for verses 2 and 4.

1 The hands of Christ, the caring hands,
    they nailed them to a cross of wood;
    the feet that climbed the desert road
    and brought the news of peace with God,
    they pierced them through.

2 The kingly Christ, the saviour-king,
    they ringed his head with briars woven;
    the lips that freely spoke of heaven,
    that told the world of sins forgiven,
    they mocked with wine.

3 Too late for life, in death too late
    they tried to maim him with a spear;
    for sacrilege they could not bear –
    the sabbath comes, so they must tear
    the heart from God.

4 To him be praise, all praise to him
    who died upon the cross of pain;
    whose agonies were not in vain –
    for Christ the Lord is risen again
    and brings us joy!

Michael Perry

Words: © Michael Perry / Jubilate Hymns. Music: © Simon Beckley / Jubilate Hymns. Music arr: © John Barnard / Jubilate Hymns.
USA © 1982 by Hope Publishing Company, Carol Stream, IL 60188

82 The Lord is here

SIBFORD FERRIS

John Barnard

1 The Lord is here. His pro-mised word is ev - er -
2 The Lord is here. Where Christ is come his Spi - rit
3 The Lord is here. He comes in peace, with bless-ings
4 The Lord is here. To ev - ery soul this gift of

- more the same: him-self to be where two or three are gath-ered
too is there with all who raise the song of praise or breathe the
from a - bove, by pledge and sign of bread and wine to fold us
grace be given, to walk the way of Christ to - day and share the

in his____ name.
voice of____ prayer.
in his____ love.

life of____ heaven.

1 The Lord is here.
      His promised word
   is evermore the same:
      himself to be
   where two or three
      are gathered in his name.

2 The Lord is here.
      Where Christ is come
   his Spirit too is there
      with all who raise
   the song of praise
      or breathe the voice of prayer.

3 The Lord is here.
      He comes in peace,
   with blessings from above,
      by pledge and sign
   of bread and wine
      to fold us in his love.

4 The Lord is here.
      To every soul
   this gift of grace be given,
      to walk the way
   of Christ today
      and share the life of heaven.

Timothy Dudley-Smith

83　The Lord's Day

Olajide Olude
arr A C Lovelace

1　Je - sus, we　want to meet　on　this thy　ho - ly day;
2　We kneel in　awe and fear　on　this thy　ho - ly day;
3　Thy bless - ing,　Lord, we seek　on　this thy　ho - ly day;
4　Our minds we　de - di - cate　on　this thy　ho - ly day;

we　ga - ther　round thy throne　on　this thy　ho - ly day.
pray God to　teach us here　on　this thy　ho - ly day.
give joy of　thy vic - to - ry　on　this thy　ho - ly day.
heart and soul　con - se - crate　on　this thy　ho - ly day.

Thou　art our　heaven - ly friend;　hear our prayers as　they as - cend;
Save us and　cleanse our hearts,　lead and guide our　acts of praise,
Through grace a - lone　are we saved;　in thy flock may　we be found;
Ho - ly　Spi - rit,　make us whole;　bless the ser - mon　in this place;

look in - to our hearts and minds to - day,　on　this thy　ho - ly day.
and our faith from seed to　flo - wer raise　on　this thy　ho - ly day.
let the mind of Christ a - bide in us　on　this thy　ho - ly day.
and as we go,　lead us, Lord;　we shall be thine　ev - er - more.

Optional drumbeat patterns

1 Jesus, we want to meet
    on this thy holy day;
  we gather round thy throne
    on this thy holy day.
  Thou art our heavenly friend;
  hear our prayers as they ascend;
  look into our hearts and minds today,
    on this thy holy day.

2 We kneel in awe and fear
    on this thy holy day;
  pray God to teach us here
    on this thy holy day.
  Save us and cleanse our hearts,
  lead and guide our acts of praise,
  and our faith from seed to flower raise
    on this thy holy day.

3 Thy blessing, Lord, we seek
    on this thy holy day;
  give joy of thy victory
    on this thy holy day.
  Through grace alone are we saved;
  in thy flock may we be found;
  let the mind of Christ abide in us
    on this thy holy day.

4 Our minds we dedicate
    on this thy holy day;
  heart and soul consecrate
    on this thy holy day.
  Holy Spirit, make us whole;
  bless the sermon in this place;
  and as we go, lead us, Lord;
    we shall be thine evermore.

B Adebisin
from Nigerian by Olajide Olude

84   Then the glory

NOW

Carl F Schalk

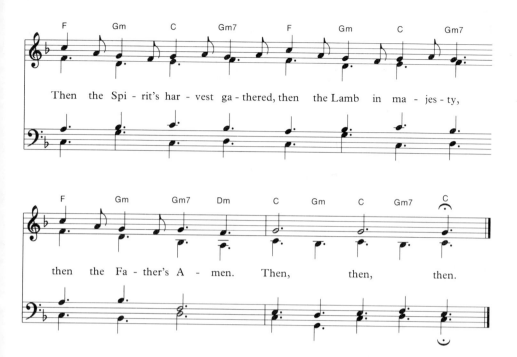

Then the Spi - rit's har - vest ga - thered, then the Lamb in ma - jes - ty,

then the Fa - ther's A - men. Then, then, then.

Then the glory,
then the rest,
then the sabbath peace unbroken;

Then the garden,
then the throne,
then the crystal river flowing;

Then the splendour,
then the life,
then the new creation singing;

Then the marriage,
then the love,
then the feast of joy unending;

Then the knowing,
then the light,
then the ultimate adventure;

Then the Spirit's harvest gathered,
then the Lamb in majesty,
then the Father's Amen.

Then, then, then.

Jaroslav J Vajda

The song No. 58 entitled 'Now the silence' can be used in conjunction with this song

85 There's a spirit in the air

LAUDS

John Wilson

Unis. 1 There's a spi - rit in the air, tell - ing Chris - tians
Harm. 2 Lose your shy - ness, find your tongue, tell___ the world what
Unis. 4 Still the Spi - rit gives us light, see - ing wrong and

ev - ery - where:___ Praise the love that Christ re - vealed,___
God has done:___ God___ in Christ has come___ to stay.___
set - ting right:___ God___ in Christ has come___ to stay.___

liv - ing, work - ing, in___ our world.___
Live___ to - mor - row's life___ to -
Live___ to - mor - row's life___ to -

*Small notes keyboard only.

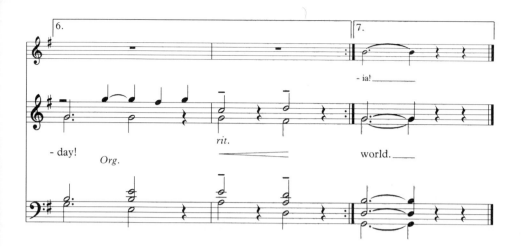

1 There's a spirit in the air,
    telling Christians everywhere:
 Praise the love that Christ revealed,
    living, working, in our world.

2 Lose your shyness, find your tongue,
    tell the world what God has done:
 God in Christ has come to stay.
    Live tomorrow's life today!

3* When believers break the bread,
    when a hungry child is fed,
 praise the love that Christ revealed,
    living, working, in our world.

4 Still the Spirit gives us light,
    seeing wrong and setting right:
 God in Christ has come to stay.
    Live tomorrow's life today!

5* When a stranger's not alone,
    where the homeless find a home,
 praise the love that Christ revealed,
    living, working, in our world.

6 May the Spirit fill our praise,
    guide our thoughts and change our ways:
 God in Christ has come to stay.
    Live tomorrow's life today!

7 There's a Spirit in the air,
    calling people everywhere:
 Praise the love that Christ revealed,
    living, working, in our world.

Brian Wren

*Verses 3 and 5 may be sung by choir or soloist only

86 The song of the supper

AFTON WATER

Scottish folk song
arr Allan Wicks

1 The time was ear - ly eve - ning, the___ place a room up -
2 The com - pa - ny of Je - sus had___ met to share a
3 'The bread and bo - dy bro - ken, the___ wine and blood out -
4 On both sides of the ta - ble, on___ both sides of the
5 Lord Je - sus, now a - mong us, con - firm our faith's in -

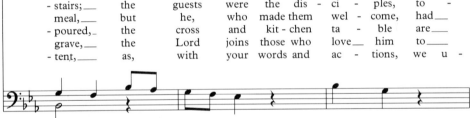

- stairs;___ the guests were the dis - ci - ples, to -
meal,___ but he, who made them wel - come, had___
- poured,___ the cross and kit - chen ta - ble are___
grave,___ the Lord joins those who love___ him to___
- tent,___ as, with your words and ac - tions, we u -

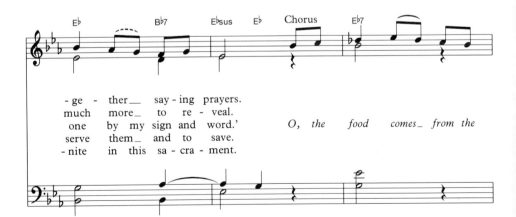

- ge - ther___ say - ing prayers.
much more___ to re - veal.
one by my sign and word.'
serve them___ and to save.
- nite in this sa - cra - ment.

O, the food comes___ from the

ba - ker, the drink comes from the vine,____ the
words come from the Sav - iour, 'I will meet you in bread and wine.'

1   The time was early evening,
    the place a room upstairs;
    the guests were the disciples,
    together saying prayers.

> *O, the food comes from the baker,*
> *the drink comes from the vine,*
> *the words come from the Saviour,*
> *'I will meet you in bread and wine.'*

2   The company of Jesus
    had met to share a meal,
  but he, who made them welcome,
    had much more to reveal.
      O, the food . . .

3   'The bread and body broken,
    the wine and blood outpoured,
  the cross and kitchen table
    are one by my sign and word.'
      O, the food . . .

4   On both sides of the table,
    on both sides of the grave,
  the Lord joins those who love him
    to serve them and to save.
      O, the food . . .

5   Lord Jesus, now among us,
    confirm our faith's intent,
  as, with your words and actions,
    we unite in this sacrament.
      O, the food . . .

John Bell and Graham Maule

Wherever possible the words of verse 3 should be sung by a solo voice

87 They killed him as a common thief

EASTERTIDE

John Dankworth

1 They killed him as a com-mon thief, they saw no King in his
(2 They) laid him in a bor-rowed tomb, they saw the death in his

eyes;_____ they drew his royal re - deem-ing blood be -
eyes;_____ they rolled the door of hea - vy stone be -

- low the dark - en - ing skies:_____ then Christ, Je - sus the
- low the sor - row-ing skies:_____ then Christ, Je - sus the

Lord, sound - ed a loud tri - umph - ant cry –_____ his
King, stood a-mong all, the Lord of Life;_____ and

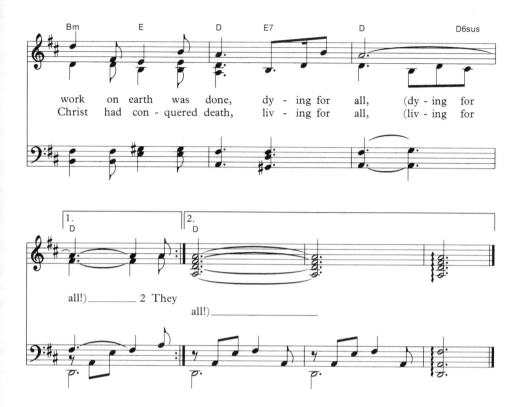

work on earth was done, dy - ing for all, (dy - ing for
Christ had con - quered death, liv - ing for all, (liv - ing for

all!)⎯⎯⎯⎯ 2 They
all!)⎯⎯⎯⎯

1 They killed him as a common thief,
 they saw no King in his eyes;
 they drew his royal redeeming blood
 below the darkening skies:
  then Christ,
  Jesus the Lord,
   sounded a loud triumphant cry –
 his work on earth was done,
  dying for all!

2 They laid him in a borrowed tomb,
 they saw the death in his eyes;
 they rolled the door of heavy stone
 below the sorrowing skies:
  then Christ,
  Jesus the King,
   stood among all, the Lord of Life;
 and Christ had conquered death,
  living for all!

Paul Wigmore

88 Three days on

THREE DAYS ON

David Iliff

1 I found him cra-dled in a lamp-lit barn, his mo-ther
2 I heard him laugh-ing in the tem-ple court the day his
3 I saw him weep-ing o-ver sin and death, the sick and

Ma - ry rocked him; the child was God they hung to - day on a
par - ents lost him; the boy was God they hung to - day and I'll
dy - ing round him; the man was God they hung to - day on a

big high cross and they mocked him there: *One day on, the tomb is*
ne - ver know what it cost him there: *Two days on, the tomb is*
big high cross when I found him there. *Three days on, the tomb is*

si - lent, one day on,__ all hea-ven weeps; one day on,__ and e - ven
si - lent, two days on,__ all hea-ven weeps; two days on,__ and still the
o - pen! Three days on,__ the loud re - frain: Christ has died__ and Christ is

star - light hid from Christ___ who sleeps
star - light hid from Christ___ who sleeps
ri - sen, Christ will   come___   a - gain!

1   I found him cradled in a lamp-lit barn,
      his mother Mary rocked him;
   the child was God they hung today
      on a big high cross and they mocked him there:

      One day on, the tomb is silent,
        one day on, all heaven weeps;
      one day on, and even starlight
        hid from Christ who sleeps . . .

2   I heard him laughing in the temple court
      the day his parents lost him;
   the boy was God they hung today
      and I'll never know what it cost him there:

      Two days on, the tomb is silent,
        two days on, all heaven weeps;
      two days on, and still the starlight
        hid from Christ who sleeps . . .

3   I saw him weeping over sin and death,
      the sick and dying round him;
   the man was God they hung today
      on a big high cross when I found him there.

      Three days on, the tomb is open!
      Three days on, the loud refrain:
      Christ has died and Christ is risen,
      Christ will come again!

                  Paul Wigmore

89 'Tis the gift to be simple

SHAKER SONG

arr William Llewellyn

First time S. & A. (or Full)
Second time T. & B. (or Full)

mp

1 'Tis the gift to be sim-ple, 'tis the gift to be free, 'tis the

gift to come down where you ought to be; and when we find our-selves in the

2nd time **to Coda** ⊕

place just right, 'twill be in the val - ley of love and de-light.

Full

2 When true sim - pli-ci-ty is gained, to bow and to bend we

shan't be a-shamed; to turn, turn will be our de-light, till by

turn-ing, turn-ing we come round right._____

CODA

Soprano

mf

love and de-light. When true sim - pli - ci - ty is gained, to

Alto/Tenor

mf

love and de-light. When true sim - pli - ci - ty is

Bass

mf

love and de-light. When true sim -

cresc.

mf

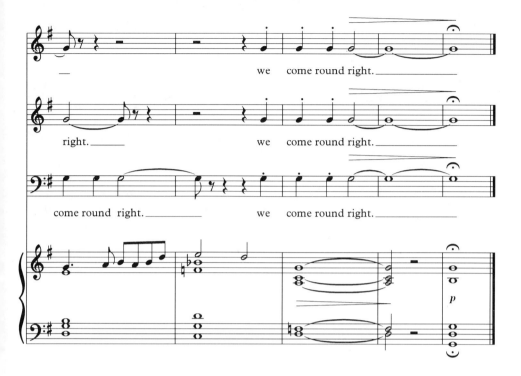

we come round right.

right. we come round right.

come round right. we come round right.

1 'Tis the gift to be simple,'tis the gift to be free,
   'tis the gift to come down where you ought to be;
 and when we find ourselves in the place just right,
   'twill be in the valley of love and delight.

2 When true simplicity is gained,
   to bow and to bend we shan't be ashamed;
 to turn, turn will be our delight,
   till by turning, turning we come round right.

Anon

90   We cannot measure how you heal

YE BANKS AND BRAES

Scottish traditional melody
arr John Bell

1 We can - not mea - sure how_ you heal_ or ans - wer
2 The pain that will_ not go_ a - way,_ the guilt_ that
3 So some have come_ who need_ your help_ and some_ have

ev - ery suffer - er's prayer, yet_ we be - lieve_ your
clings_ from things_ long past, the_ fear of what_ the
come_ to make_ a - mends, as_ hands which shaped and

grace_ res - ponds where faith_ and doubt_ u - nite_ to
fu - ture holds, are pre - sent as_ if meant to
saved_ the world_ are pre - sent in_ the touch_ of

care. Your hands, though blood - ied on the cross, sur - vive_ to
last. But pre - sent too_ is love which tends_ the hurt_ we
friends. Lord, let your Spi - rit meet us here_ to mend the

hold__ and heal__ and__ warn,__ to__ car - ry all__ through
ne - ver hope__ to__ find,__ the__ pri - vate a - gon -
bo - dy, mind__ and__ soul,__ to__ dis - en - tan - gle

death to life__ and cra - dle__ child - ren yet__ un - born.
- ies__ in - side,__ the me - mo - ries__ that haunt the mind.
peace from pain__ and make__ your bro - ken peo - ple whole.

1 We cannot measure how you heal
    or answer every sufferer's prayer,
  yet we believe your grace responds
    where faith and doubt unite to care.
  Your hands, though bloodied on the cross,
    survive to hold and heal and warn,
  to carry all through death to life
    and cradle children yet unborn.

2 The pain that will not go away,
    the guilt that clings from things long past,
  the fear of what the future holds,
    are present as if meant to last.
  But present too is love which tends
    the hurt we never hope to find,
  the private agonies inside,
    the memories that haunt the mind.

3 So some have come who need your help
    and some have come to make amends,
  as hands which shaped and saved the world
    are present in the touch of friends.
  Lord, let your Spirit meet us here
    to mend the body, mind and soul,
  to disentangle peace from pain
    and make your broken people whole.

John Bell and Graham Maule

91 We do not know how to pray

PRAYER CANTICLE

Erik Routley

*The Antiphon may be sung in unison and the verses by one or two soloists.
Alternatively, male and female voices may be contrasted, using either unison or solo.

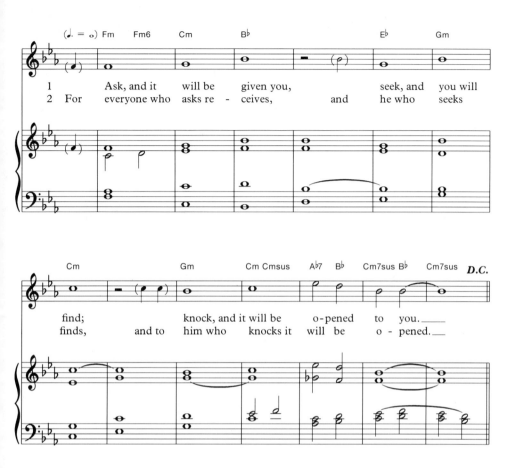

We do not know how to pray as we ought,
but the Spirit himself intercedes for us
with sighs too deep for words.

1   Ask, and it will be given you,
        seek, and you will find;
    knock, and it will be opened to you.
        We do not know . . .

2   For everyone who asks receives,
        and he who seeks finds,
    and to him who knocks it will be opened.
        We do not know . . .

Alan Luff
from Romans 8: 26
and Luke 11: 9–10

92 We remembered on the road

EASTER NIGHT

Cyril Taylor

1 We re-mem-bered on the road, when the
(2 Some-one) joins us on the way, in the
(3 'Gra-cious) stran-ger, be our guest, share the

sun was set-ting, all the glo - ry Je - sus showed, great-est
twi - light walk-ing, and the chan - ges dark to day, of the
joy we owe you.' Then he broke the bread and blessed –'Lord, it's

past for - get-ting, now re - ced - ing, sink-ing fast, with the
pro - phets talk-ing, 'God has pro - mised life from death, joy like
you! We know you.' And he van - ished from our gaze, now to

day-light dy - ing, and our hopes de-ceived at last, with his bo - dy ly - ing.
Spring re-turn-ing.' Faith and hope, the Spi-rit's breath, set our hearts a-burn-ing.
leave us ne - ver, ris - en Christ of end-less days, with us now and ev - er.

2 Some-one
3 'Gra-cious

1 We remembered on the road,
    when the sun was setting,
all the glory Jesus showed,
    greatest past forgetting,
now receding, sinking fast,
    with the daylight dying,
and our hopes deceived at last,
    with his body lying.

2 Someone joins us on the way,
    in the twilight walking,
and the changes dark to day,
    of the prophets talking,
'God has promised life from death,
    joy like Spring returning.'
Faith and hope, the Spirit's breath,
    set our hearts a-burning.

3 'Gracious stranger, be our guest,
    share the joy we owe you.'
Then he broke the bread and blessed –
    'Lord, it's you! We know you.'
And he vanished from our gaze,
    now to leave us never,
risen Christ of endless days,
    with us now and ever.

Emily Chisholm

93 We will lay our burden down

LAYING DOWN

John Bell

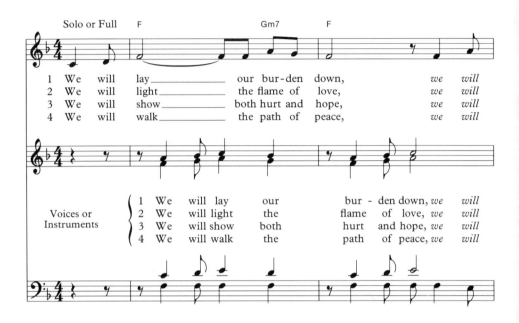

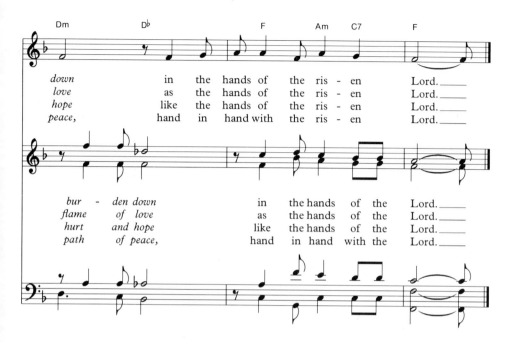

1 We will lay our burden down,
  we will lay our burden down,
  we will lay our burden down
    in the hands of the risen Lord.

2 We will light the flame of love,
  we will light the flame of love,
  we will light the flame of love
    as the hands of the risen Lord.

3 We will show both hurt and hope,
  we will show both hurt and hope,
  we will show both hurt and hope
    like the hands of the risen Lord.

4 We will walk the path of peace,
  we will walk the path of peace,
  we will walk the path of peace
    hand in hand with the risen Lord.

John Bell and Graham Maule

94 Were you there when they crucified my Lord?

WERE YOU THERE?

American spiritual melody
arr Francis B Westbrook

1 Were you there when they cru - ci - fied my Lord? (were you
2 Were you there when they nailed him to the tree? (were you
3 Were you there when they laid him in the tomb? (were you
4 Were you there when he rose up from the tomb? (were you

there) Were you there___ when they cru - ci - fied my
there) Were you there___ when they nailed him to the
there) Were you there___ when they laid him in the
there) Were you there___ when he rose up from the

Lord? (when they cru - ci - fied my Lord?)
tree? (when they nailed him to the tree?)
tomb? (when they laid him in the tomb?)
tomb? (when he rose up from the tomb?)

some-times it cau - ses me to trem-ble, trem-ble, trem-ble; Were you there____ when they cru - ci - fied my Lord?____

1   Were you there when they crucified my Lord?
     Were you there when they crucified my Lord?

*   O, sometimes it causes me to tremble, tremble, tremble;*
*   Were you there when they crucified my Lord?*

2   Were you there when they nailed him to the tree?
     Were you there when they nailed him to the tree?

*   O, sometimes it causes me to tremble, tremble, tremble;*
*   Were you there when they nailed him to the tree?*

3   Were you there when they laid him in the tomb?
     Were you there when they laid him in the tomb?

*   O, sometimes it causes me to tremble, tremble, tremble;*
*   Were you there when they laid him in the tomb?*

4   Were you there when he rose up from the tomb?
     Were you there when he rose up from the tomb?

*   O, sometimes it causes me to tremble, tremble, tremble;*
*   Were you there when he rose up from the tomb?*

Traditional Spiritual

95 What wondrous love is this

WONDROUS LOVE

Harmonisation by Carlton R Young

Unison

1 What won-drous love is this, O my soul, O my soul! What
2 To God and to the Lamb, I will sing, I will sing, to
3 And when from death I'm free, I'll sing on, I'll sing on, and

won-drous love is this, O my soul! What won-drous love is this that
God and to the Lamb, I will sing. To God and to the Lamb who
when from death I'm free, I'll sing on. And when from death I'm free, I'll

caused the Lord of bliss to lay a - side his crown for my
is the great I AM, while mil - lions join the theme, I will
sing and joy - ful be, and through e - ter - ni - ty I'll sing

soul, for my soul, to lay a - side his crown for my soul.
sing, I will sing, while mil - lions join the theme I will sing.
on, I'll sing on, and through e - ter - ni - ty I'll sing on.

Keyboard and guitar should not sound together. The following harmonization may accompany unison singing.

1 What wondrous love is this, O my soul, O my soul!
   What wondrous love is this, O my soul!
   What wondrous love is this that caused the Lord of bliss
       to lay aside his crown for my soul, for my soul,
       to lay aside his crown for my soul.

2 To God and to the Lamb, I will sing, I will sing,
       to God and to the Lamb, I will sing.
   To God and to the Lamb who is the great I AM,
       while millions join the theme, I will sing, I will sing,
       while millions join the theme I will sing.

3 And when from death I'm free, I'll sing on, I'll sing on,
       and when from death I'm free, I'll sing on.
   And when from death I'm free, I'll sing and joyful be,
       and through eternity I'll sing on, I'll sing on,
       and through eternity I'll sing on.

American folk hymn

96　When we are down you raise us up

SONGS OF PRAISE

Robert Prizeman

1 When we are down you raise us up, _____ when
2 When we are bound you set us free, _____ when

we are weak you make us strong; _____ when
we are wrong you put us right; _____ when

we are lost you_ bring us_ hope, our Strength, our Sav - iour_
we are blind you_ let_ us_ see our world's Re - deem - er_

and_ our Song: to God be glo – ry all_ our days!
and_ our Light: in Christ we come with songs of praise!

OPTIONAL ADDITIONAL KEYBOARD PART

1 When we are down you raise us up,
   when we are weak you make us strong;
 when we are lost you bring us hope,
   our Strength, our Saviour and our Song:
   to God be glory all our days!

2 When we are bound you set us free,
   when we are wrong you put us right;
 when we are blind you let us see
   our world's Redeemer and our Light:
   in Christ we come with songs of praise!

Christopher Idle

97 Whitsuntide round

Kenneth Simpson

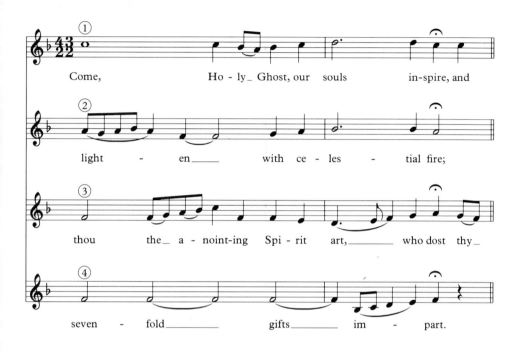

Come, Holy Ghost, our souls inspire,
    and lighten with celestial fire;
thou the anointing Spirit art,
    who dost thy sevenfold gifts impart.

John Cosin

Words and music: Reproduced from *50 Sacred Canons and Rounds* (Ed. Kenneth Simpson) By permission of Novello
& Company Limited

98 When you prayed beneath the trees

KELVINGROVE

Scottish traditional melody
arr John Bell

1 When you prayed be - neath the trees, it was for me, O Lord;__
2 When their tri - umph looked com - plete, it was for me, O Lord,__
3 When you stum - bled up the road, you walked for me, O Lord,__
4 When you spoke with king - ly power, it was for me, O Lord,__

when you cried up - on your knees, how could it be, O Lord?__
when it seemed like your de - feat, they could not see, O Lord!__
when you took your dead - ly load, that hea - vy tree, O Lord;__
in that dread and des - tined hour, you made me free, O Lord;__

When in blood and sweat and tears__ you dis-missed your fi - nal fears,__
When you faced the mob a - lone__ you were si - lent as a stone,__
When they lift - ed you on high,__ and they nailed you up to die,__
earth and hea - ven heard you shout,__ death and hell were put to rout,__

Harmonies may be hummed

when you faced the sol-diers' spears, you stood for me, O Lord.
and a tree be-came your throne; you came for me, O Lord.
and when dark-ness filled the sky, it was for me, O Lord.
for the grave could not hold out; you are for me, O Lord.

1 When you prayed beneath the trees, it was for me, O Lord;
   when you cried upon your knees, how could it be, O Lord?
      When in blood and sweat and tears
      you dismissed your final fears,
   when you faced the soldiers' spears, you stood for me, O Lord.

2 When their triumph looked complete, it was for me, O Lord,
   when it seemed like your defeat, they could not see, O Lord!
      When you faced the mob alone
      you were silent as a stone,
   and a tree became your throne; you came for me, O Lord.

3 When you stumbled up the road, you walked for me, O Lord,
   when you took your deadly load, that heavy tree, O Lord;
      When they lifted you on high,
      and they nailed you up to die,
   and when darkness filled the sky, it was for me, O Lord.

4 When you spoke with kingly power, it was for me, O Lord,
   in that dread and destined hour, you made me free, O Lord;
      earth and heaven heard you shout,
      death and hell were put to rout,
   for the grave could not hold out; you are for me, O Lord.

Christopher Idle

99 With wonder, Lord

MANTON HOLLOW

John Barnard

1 With   won - der, Lord, we   see   your   works,_____ we
(2 With) won - der, Lord, we   see   your   works,_____ and
(3 The)   stars that   fill   the   skies   a - bove,_____ the
(4 We)   praise your works, yet   we   our - selves_____ are
(5 All)   you   have   made   is   ours   to   rule,_____ the

see the beau - ty   you have   made;_____ this earth, the skies, all things that
child-like   in   our   joy we   sing_____ to   praise you, bless you, mak - er,
sun and moon which give our   light,_____ are   your de - sign - ing for   our
works of   won - der made by   you;_____ not   far from you in   all   we
birds and beasts   at   will to   tame,_____ all   things to   or - der for the

1–4.

are   in beau - ty   made.
Lord   of   ev - ery - thing.
use   and our de - light.
are   and all we   do.

5.

2 With
3 The
4 We
5 All

glo - ry of your name.

Possible scheme of performance
    verse 1 – Upper voices/Treble voices
    verse 2 – Men
    verse 3 – All
    verse 4 – Choir Upper voices/Treble voices
    verse 5 – All (with descant)

use and our de - light. 4 We

praise your works, yet we our - selves ____ are works of won-der made by you; ____ not

far from you in all we are and all we do. 5 All

OPTIONAL DESCANT FOR VERSE 5

(Ah)

1 With wonder, Lord, we see your works,
we see the beauty you have made;
this earth, the skies, all things that are in beauty made.

2 With wonder, Lord, we see your works,
and child-like in our joy we sing
to praise you, bless you, maker, Lord of everything.

3 The stars that fill the skies above,
the sun and moon which give our light,
are your designing for our use and our delight.

4 We praise your works, yet we ourselves
are works of wonder made by you;
not far from you in all we are and all we do.

5 All you have made is ours to rule,
the birds and beasts at will to tame,
all things to order for the glory of your name.

Brian Foley,
from Psalm 8

100   You shall go out with joy

TREES OF THE FIELD

Steffi Geiser Rubin

You shall go out with joy and be led forth with peace, and the moun-tains and the hills shall break forth be-fore you. There'll be shouts of joy and the trees of the field shall clap, shall clap their hands, and the trees of the field shall clap their hands, and the

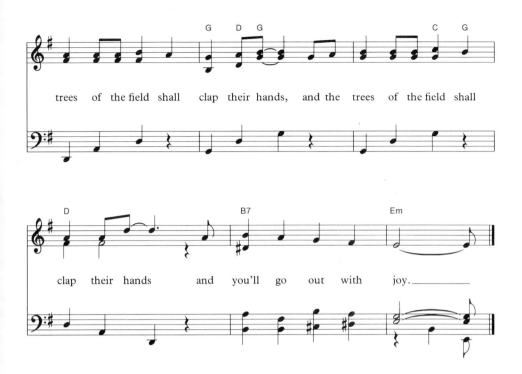

trees of the field shall clap their hands, and the trees of the field shall

clap their hands and you'll go out with joy.

You shall go out with joy
and be led forth with peace,
and the mountains and the hills shall
break forth before you.
There'll be shouts of joy
and the trees of the field
shall clap, shall clap their hands,
and the trees of the field shall clap their hands,
and the trees of the field shall clap their hands,
and the trees of the field shall clap their hands
and you'll go out with joy.

S Dauermann
from Isaiah 55 v. 12

INDEX OF AUTHORS, TRANSLATORS, AND
SOURCES OF TEXTS

INDEX OF COMPOSERS, ARRANGERS, AND SOURCES OF MUSIC

An asterisk denotes a harmonization or arrangement

INDEX OF FIRST LINES, TITLES AND TUNES

A blank denotes the absence of a separate tune name.
Where titles differ from first lines, they are in italics